A Parent's Su Guide to Childhood Depression

by Susan E. Dubuque

Childswork
Childsplay

Plainview, New York

A Parent's Survival Guide to Childhood Depression

By Susan E. Dubuque

Childswork/Childsplay publishes products for mental health professionals, teachers and parents who wish to help children with their developmental, social and emotional growth. For questions, comments, or to request a free catalog describing hundreds of games, toys, books, and other counseling tools, call 1-800-962-1141.

© 1996 Childswork/Childsplay, LLC
A Guidance Channel Company
135 Dupont Street
Plainview, NY 11803

ISBN 1-882732-49-9

DEDICATION

To Nicholas. My gentle Dragon.

ACKNOWLEDGMENTS

I would like to offer a special word of thanks to the many people who helped bring this book to life.

The following are experts in their respective fields. I am appreciative for all their time and assistance. They shared information and resources, reviewed the manuscript, and ensured that I didn't say anything too terribly stupid.

Donnie Amos, R.P.H., Pharmacist
Ami Butta, M.S.W., School Social Worker.
Phyllis R. Cazares, Ph.D., Clinical Psychologist
Gerardo Crichigno, M.D., Child Psychiatrist
Robert Cross, M.D., Family Practice Physician
James Edwards, M.D., Child Psychiatrist
Lisa Hand, M.D., Child Psychiatrist
Lisa Hudson, M.Ed., School Psychologist/Certified Guidance Counselor
Livia Jansen, Ph.D., Clinical Psychologist
Terry Jones, Parent Coordinator, Parents and Children Coping Together
Leslie Kaplan, Ed.D., School Administrator
Rebecca Reynolds, R.N., Psychiatric Nurse
Mary Jane Sale, Ph.D., Clinical Psychologist
Carolyn South, M.Ed., Licensed Professional Counselor
Eileen Stellefson, M.P.H., R.D., C.E.D.S., Registered Dietitian
Deveron Timberlake, Program Coordinator, AIM-Awareness
Evonne Weinhaus, M.A., Licensed Counselor

I am especially grateful to Ami Butta for suggesting the Turtle image. In my first draft, I referred to these characters as a Rabbit and Dragon. The Turtle is definitely stronger and more accurate.

In addition to being a member of my panel of clinical experts, Evonne Weinhaus served as my writing mentor. She offered practical suggestions for the book, as well as tons of encouragement and support as I attempted my first venture into the world of publishing.

Terry Jones and Deveron Timberlake really deserve credit for giving this book a jump-start. They shared some of the most valuable resource materials and contacts with me.

I would like to thank my friends and colleagues who patiently listened to me babble on endlessly about this project, and who reviewed draft after draft — proofreading, critiquing, and cheering me along the way.

William Baskervill
Margaret Bonner
Charles Breindel, Ph.D.
Chatra Burford
Marty Campanello
Sidney Cristol
Lyne Doyle
Gail Kent
Dorothy Knox
Roger Neathawk
Philippa Osdene
Leslie Rennolds

It was Bill Baskervill who encouraged me to include all the juicy personal stuff so that my book wouldn't be dry and wooden. Those sections ended up being the most fun to write.

My friend Margo Bonner was my sounding board. She could probably recite 95 percent of this book from memory.

Most of all, I would like to extend a heartfelt thanks to Dr. Livia Jansen. She helped me believe in myself as a writer and, more importantly, as a competent mother. Nicholas and I both owe her more than she'll ever know — at least until now.

FOREWORD

As many as six million children and adolescents in the United States—about 10 percent of our children—are depressed. Imagine every child at every desk in every classroom of every school in five states—the numbers are staggering. The American Medical Association recently reported the grim fact that mental disorders have become the leading disability among 10- to 18-year-olds in this country. And yet most of these children are not receiving treatment.

Susan Dubuque's book can be instrumental in changing this trend. Depressed children and their families are often confused, frightened, and isolated. They may be overwhelmed by stress, cut off from needed support, and uncertain where to turn for help. This honest and courageous book by a mother who has been through the gauntlet of depression with her child should give hope and direction to those who are still foundering.

With warmth, love, and humor Ms. Dubuque recounts the story of her journey, of her son's struggle, and shows us the warning signals and guideposts along the way. She points out the pitfalls in the diagnosis of depression and explains why even the professionals have underdiagnosed the condition for so many years.

In Chapter Seven, Ms. Dubuque provides parents with a clear and concise review of the various treatment options available. Treatment today can involve multiple different approaches, each directed toward a particular problem or contributing factor. Cognitive therapy is directed toward distortions and disturbances of thinking that characterize depression, social skills training toward improving the child's ability to enjoy good relationships, and family therapy is aimed at correcting any family problems that could be contributing to the child's distress. A new approach we are using in my practice involves teaching mindfulness meditation and stress management skills to parents. In the next phase of our research we will be including the children in the training, teaching them a simple form of mindfulness meditation along with their parents. We are also helping parents identify their personality styles and parenting styles according to a system called Enneagram. This is proving to be a very powerful tool for self-understanding and change.

As research into the causes of childhood depression continues, as innovative treatment approaches appear, I hope we will see earlier and more effective care for this serious problem. I congratulate Susan Dubuque for her courageous and generous book, and I trust that it will bring comfort and guidance to any families in need.

—Lawrence L. Kerns, M.D.
Author of *Helping Your Depressed Child*

CONTENTS

INTRODUCTION

"What do you want from me? I don't want to go out and play with the other kids. They're all dweebs. Besides they don't want to play with me anyway. They all hate me."

"School's a drag. My teachers are a drag. Life sucks. Sometimes I don't get it. I'm a kid. And everyone expects me to be laughing and having a great time. Well ha, ha. What a big laugh."

"Sometimes it's like everything is closing in on me. Once I crawled out the window to get away. Then there are times I wish everything would close in around me. That way I'd be safe."

"Some days I feel OK. Then it comes over me. Like a big wet, wool blanket that just sticks to me and weighs me down. Just moving is work. All I want to do is crawl back in bed and sleep for a long time. I mean a really long time."

"I hate when she asks me, 'How was your day?' 'What did you learn?' It's like she's grilling me. And I just want to be left alone for a while. It's too much, too soon. Go away."

All right. I made these comments up. But they're based on reality. I know for sure because my son-the-expert says so. This is how children who are depressed really feel. That is, when they are able to open up and express their feelings. But that's the problem. Most of the time they aren't.

I'm not an M.D. or a Ph.D. I'm just a M.O.M. Specifically, I'm the mom of an eleven-year-old child who suffers from depression.

My journey into the world of testing, psychotherapy, antidepressants, and mile-long guilt trips actually started in 1986. No, let's make that 1984, to really give you the total picture.

Nicholas was the cutest baby ever born. Even as a newborn. And we all know that a "cute newborn" is an oxymoron. But he was cute. A head full of straight, thick hair. Intense dark eyes. From day one his eyes were nearly black. That should have been a clue.

By two years of age, he had turned into an energetic tow-head—a blond so white that it looks like it came from a peroxide bottle. He could climb to the top of a bookshelf before you could count to three. It drove his babysitters nuts. Personally, I thought he was quite industrious.

At two-and-a-half we proudly enrolled our first-born in the Montessori School. And three days later the phone calls and teacher meetings started. Another omen perhaps. Lack of social development. Poor peer relations. Refuses to be touched. Won't listen. It seemed the teacher was actually afraid of my 24-pound, doe-eyed boy. Amazing.

By the time Nicholas was three, we were visiting the first of a string of psychologists, social workers, and various and sundry mental health professionals. The testing experience was a trip. After the first clinician plucked Nicholas off the mini-blinds, removed the trash can from his head, and conducted her assessment, she unequivocally reported that he was too young to get a definitive diagnosis. Of course, this finding was somewhat of a mystery since he was the same age at the time the appointment was scheduled as he was at the time of testing. It would have been a whole lot easier and a whole lot cheaper to tell us he was too young before we dropped $300 into the kitty.

Age five. A second trip to the psychologist for testing. This time the results are unquestionable. The child lacks discipline. Perhaps if we take a course...

Next stop—the psychiatrist, to see if Ritalin® will help. She looks at the most recent test results and assures us that this kid doesn't need medication. Just better parents. Of course, this astute diagnosis is made while my son is dismantling her waiting area. Finally, she agrees to actually look at my child—just to humor the "histrionic mother"—that would be me. In about four minutes she emerges from the office, looking a little pale. "This child has marked neurological problems." No kidding. What do you think we've been trying to tell you for the past hour?

OK. So we start the Ritalin. No, actually, we try to save 60¢ a month and use the generic brand. The kid looks like a zombie. A kindly, smart pharmacist suggests that we try the brandname. There really is a difference. In fact, in three days the teachers are noticing a real improvement. Hooray. We think the perfect solution is a 10 mg. yellow pill. Wrong. Some days are terrific. Others are hell.

The culminating experience happens at age 10. With full support from our therapist—this time a wonderful clinical psychologist to whom I will always be grateful—we had Nicholas evaluated once more. The objective was to determine if the histrionic mom—that's me, remember—was correct in her assessment that this kid "looks depressed." The night before we're scheduled to review the test results, Nicholas holes up in a closet, presses a toy gun to his head, and says, "If it was real, I'd use it." So who's histrionic now? The psychologist tells us, no surprises here, that our son is suffering from serious depression, and we'd better get help for him immediately.

Hallelujah. For the first time we have a name for this wild and crazy roller-coaster ride—and with it comes the hope of treatment.

Prozac. The news is overloaded with the horror stories of people killing themselves while on this drug. Then I read about the flip side. Wonder drug. It turns torn, ravaged lives into wholesome, productive ones. We're scared to death. But the closet scene was no picnic either. The doctor promises to see him every week. We'll monitor this child like the Three-Mile Island start-up after the near-meltdown.

The change is slow. Subtle. No miracle cure here. But the curve is finally headed in the right direction. We go three steps forward and one step back. Beats the heck out of one forward and six back. I'll take it.

It's now one year later, and Nicholas and I have decided to write a book about childhood depression. Nicholas' first question was, "Can we be on a talk show?" I assured him that he wasn't that sick.

Don't expect this to be a depressing tale about some sad kid and his exhausted mother. In fact, this is one of the most fun, exciting projects I've ever worked on.

It's a book of information. I sifted through every piece of literature that I could find on the subject of childhood depression. I interviewed parents, teachers, social workers, psychologists, psychiatrists, family doctors, and, of course, children. My intention was not to create an anthology of childhood depression, but rather to boil down the mass of information and make sense of this incredibly complex subject.

It's a book of practical ideas. Perhaps the most valuable part of my research was asking other parents, "What have you tried?" Moms and dads can be amazingly resourceful and creative when it comes to helping their children. I also included a resource guide listing associations, books, games, and other materials that you might find helpful.

It's a book of hope. Hope that others will learn more about this pervasive, yet misunderstood emotional problem. Depression can wreak havoc not only on the child, but the entire family. There are no easy answers or ready solutions. But there are new treatment options available today that didn't exist a few years ago. There are strategies that have worked for others. And there is comfort in knowing you're not alone, and you're not to blame.

It's a book of sharing. I was impressed by the openness of the parents and children I interviewed. They willingly shared their fears, failures, successes, and dreams. And the professionals, who shared their time and expertise—not for financial gain, but with a genuine desire to help. Most of all, this book reflects my son Nicholas' willingness to share his story. For it was with his help that I came to better understand the inner workings of a depressed child's mind and heart.

The pages you are about to read reflect our exploration into the world of childhood depression. Come along for the ride. You'll learn what childhood depression is and what it isn't. When you're finished, you'll know about the various causes and treatment options, feel empowered in dealing with schools, and learn how to survive as a parent and how to support your child along the way.

Maybe it won't be such a bad ride if we take it together.

CHAPTER ONE

DEPRESSION: BEYOND SADNESS

Perhaps the best way to define depression is to explore what it is not.

Clinical depression is not a case of the blues. It's not having a bad day. Or coping with a major loss, such as the death of a parent, grandparent, or even a favorite pet. It is not a personal weakness or a character flaw. Individuals suffering from depression cannot simply "pull themselves up by their bootstraps." Depression is a form of mental illness that affects the whole body—it impacts the way one feels, thinks, and acts.

Depression is not a condition children simply outgrow. Left untreated, depression in childhood can lead to adolescent adjustment problems ranging from academic failure, to substance abuse, to suicide. And it doesn't stop there. A large proportion of adult psychiatric problems actually first appear in childhood.

As recently as the 1970s, the mental health profession thought that children were incapable of experiencing depression. Fortunately, that myth has since been dispelled. We now know that children are capable of experiencing depression with the same severity as adults.

CHAPTER TWO

WHY IS DEPRESSION SO DIFFICULT TO DETECT IN CHILDREN?

There are an estimated six million children and adolescents who are suffering from depression, yet most remain undiagnosed and untreated.

I suspect that as a society, we have a difficult time thinking of young, innocent boys and girls as being depressive. It defies every stereotype of a joyful, carefree childhood.

Perhaps a more compelling reason is that childhood depression may look different from adult depression. Depressed children may, in fact, wear two faces.

As a simple means of visualizing two manifestations of childhood depression, use your imagination and picture a "Turtle" and a "Dragon."

First, the Turtle. This child is withdrawn, quiet, and compliant. A Turtle—more often than not a girl—may be described by her parents as sensitive and shy. She may be a bit clingy and dependent and have vague physical complaints. She probably sits in the back of the classroom at school and doesn't make waves. And since the teacher has 35 other kids in the class, half of whom are bouncing off the walls, our little Turtle may be seen as a blessing, not a concern. And there goes one depressed kid, slipping through the cracks.

On the other side, there are the Dragons. Dragons—frequently boys—appear to be aggressive, angry kids. They can drive their parents, especially their moms, to distraction. They may have a difficult time getting along with friends. Dragons often act out at school and get lots of attention—from teachers, counselors, school psychologists, and administrators.

There is a tendency to dump Dragons into the ADD-ADHD basket. A child with this form of depression may indeed have an attention deficit disorder. He may be hyperactive. But depression is not simply a spin-off of ADD-ADHD. When present, it is a separate, coexisting condition—and must be treated as such. According to Dr. Lisa Hand of the Medical University of South Carolina Medical Center in Charleston, it is estimated that 60 percent of all ADD-ADHD kids have an additional emotional problem, most commonly depression or anxiety.

Dr. James Edwards, also of the Medical University of South Carolina, notes that a professional evaluation may be required to distinguish clinical depression from the demoralization and lowered self-esteem that often accompany ADD-ADHD. Treating a Dragon with Ritalin alone is a little like treating a child who has both diabetes and a broken leg with insulin. That's great for the diabetes, but what about the broken leg?

In addition to ADD-ADHD, it is not uncommon for depressed children to be labeled with Conduct Disorder, Schizophrenia, Antisocial Personality Disorder, or Adjustment Disorder.

My Turtle and Dragon illustrations are clearly oversimplifications of a very complicated mental health problem. There are many faces of depression. Children do not neatly fall into one of two categories. Turtles are not always girls; Dragons are not always boys. The same child may act like a Turtle in one situation and a Dragon in another. But this description may help to explain how and why childhood depression has not been identified as a major medical issue among parents, educators, family physicians, pediatricians, and even some mental health professionals.

Nicholas is a classic Dragon, compounded by ADHD—an attention deficit disorder with a side order of hyperactivity. He can be angry, agitated and, at times, plain old disagreeable. He can also be sweet and engaging. But the most striking characteristic that separates my child from the garden-variety ADD-ADHD kid is joylessness. Here is a child who is healthy and bright. He receives a ton of positive attention. Yet just living is painful.

The ADHD half of the equation was detected at about age seven. We found Ritalin had a miraculous impact on Nicholas' behavior and ability to focus at school. But there was no way that this drug alone could soothe his emotional wounds.

It wasn't until three years later that a battery of psychological tests revealed an underlying state of depression. Our son wasn't oppositional. He was suffering from an emotional illness.

CHAPTER THREE

TYPES OF DEPRESSION

Let's look at some of the major categories of depression and some of the terminology that you might encounter as you read and learn about this subject.

Depression in any form may be referred to as a mood disorder, affective disorder, or depressive illness.

Clinical depression is a general term that applies to any depression that is so severe and lasting that professional treatment is needed.

Major depression, also called unipolar depression, refers to a combination of emotional and physical symptoms that affects one's ability to sleep, eat, concentrate, and enjoy life. These symptoms meet established diagnostic criteria for duration and level of functional impairment.

Bouts of depression, called episodes, can occur only once or they may be recurrent. Once a child has a major episode of depression, chances are high that the problem will resurface—particularly if the child doesn't receive treatment. Dr. Maria Kovacs (1985) found that 72 percent of the children in one study had a recurrence within five years of the initial episode.

Dysthymia has the same symptoms as major depression but in a milder form. This condition is chronic, with the symptoms dragging on for two years or more in adults and for at least one year in children. While it may not be disabling, dysthymia prevents one from operating at full steam—somewhat like a low-grade fever. People who suffer from dysthymia may also have episodes of major depression. This may be referred to as double depression.

Bipolar disorder, also called manic-depression, is a less prevalent mood disorder. Bipolar illness involves cycles of depression and mania, or elation. The mood switches can occur rapidly, but more often they are gradual. During the depressive part of the cycle, one will experience the same symptoms as major depression. During the manic stage the following symptoms may be present:

- Euphoria
- Inflated self-esteem
- Rapid speech
- Disconnected thoughts
- Distractibility
- Increased energy
- Restlessness
- Poor judgment

- Inappropriate, even bizarre social behavior
- Grandiose ideas
- Irritability

According to Dr. Robert Delong, the two most important aspects of bipolar illness in children are the intensity and the cyclical nature of the symptoms. All emotional reactions are abnormally intense. The child swings between periods of silliness, giddiness, and grandiose thoughts in the manic phase, to extreme withdrawal or agitation and rage in the depressed phase.

Dr. Delong also offers an interesting description of the way children suffering from bipolar illness think. These children will show intense interest in, and may spend hours concentrating on, a particular activity. They tend to be attracted to visual-motor tasks and love to draw. They show great attention to detail, and have lots of mental energy, vivid imaginations, and rich fantasy lives.

Like major depression, bipolar disorder can be the great pretender and is often missed or misdiagnosed as Schizophrenia, Adjustment Disorder, or Conduct Disorder.

Drs. Frederick Goodwin and Kay Redfield Jamison (1990) note that bipolar illness in adolescence may be confused with antisocial personality traits. Both have elements of impulsivity, aggression, trouble with the law, and substance abuse. One difference is the presence of elation and irritability in bipolar kids. Another clue may be the relative lack of peer influence. Bipolar kids don't need to be goaded into getting into trouble. They manage quite nicely all by themselves.

Cyclothymia is a less severe form of bipolar disorder, characterized by swings between low moods (inactivity and fatigue) and high moods (energy and overconfidence).

Hypomania is characterized by a bout of manic-type symptoms that does not meet the diagnostic criteria to be labeled a true manic episode.

Seasonal affective disorder (SAD) affects about 10 million Americans. Depressive symptoms occur on a seasonal basis as the days grow shorter and improve when the days grow long again. SAD is sometimes treated with light therapy.

Anaclitic depression was a term coined by Dr. Rene Spitz in the 1940s. She studied infants who were separated from their mothers and had no substitute to provide warmth and nurturing. These babies became withdrawn and failed to grow and thrive. This form of depression is now most commonly referred to as Failure To Thrive Syndrome.

I secretly harbor a fear that Nicholas' depression will evolve into bipolar illness—which happens to run in my family. His moods resemble a sine wave. When he's off medication, the lows are even lower. With it, the highs are higher. Sometimes I wonder if I've become so accustomed to having a sullen child that I don't recognize what normal joy looks like.

CHAPTER FOUR

DEPRESSED MOOD OR CLINICAL DEPRESSION?

All children feel sadness and grief. These are normal, healthy emotions when faced with a major stress or disappointment. The death of a loved one, moving, having problems at school, coping with a serious illness or injury, divorcing parents—any of these events can send even the most well-grounded child into a tailspin. In such situations, a depressive mood would be appropriate and expected. But, it is also passing. With loving support, time heals the pain, the mood lifts, and life goes on.

Clinical depression, on the other hand, is pervasive and lasting. It affects how your child feels, thinks, and behaves. It occurs almost every day, with symptoms that seem to hang on week after week. If untreated, depression can linger for months or even years.

The American Psychiatric Association's Diagnostic and Statistical Manual of Mental Disorders (DSM-IV, 1994) provides the following criteria for major depression:

1. Depressed mood most of the day, nearly every day or, in children, this can be irritable moods.

2. Pleasure in all or most normal activities has dropped significantly.

3. Significant weight loss or gain (at least 5 percent of body weight), or in the case of a child, has not made an expected weight gain.

4. Insomnia or hypersomnia (sleeping too much).

5. Psychomotor retardation or agitation.

6. Fatigue or loss of energy.

7. Feelings of worthlessness and/or excessive guilt.

8. Diminished ability to think or concentrate, or indecisiveness.

9. Recurrent thoughts of death and/or suicide, or a suicide plan or attempt.

A patient is diagnosed with depression if:

• At least five of these symptoms are present in the same two-week period, and at least one of the symptoms is either: (1) depressed mood, or (2) loss of interest in life's pleasures.

- The symptoms are not due to bereavement or a medical condition, including the direct physiological effects of substance abuse.

- The symptoms result in an impaired function in some significant way, such as socially and occupationally.

Now let's translate this into "parent-talk."

The following questions and the Depression Checklist found on page 14 are designed to help you determine whether your child is merely in a depressed mood or suffering from clinical depression. When in doubt, it is better to err on the side of caution, and have your child evaluated.

First ask yourself the following questions:

• **How does your child look?** Slumping posture, a drooping head, bored or worried expressions, slow speech and movement, lack of eye contact—all these can indicate depression. But so can an angry face and agitated or aggressive movements.

• **What does your child say?** Depressed kids may not express being sad. When asked how they feel, they are likely to use words like bad, lousy, rotten, or gross. Bear in mind, depression can be emotionally numbing. Some children have acclimated to feeling bad and may not realize what it's like to feel good. So when they say they are OK, they may not be lying or denying their feelings, they simply may not realize that they are not OK.

• **Is your child a boy or girl?** According to Dr. Anita Gurian, you must consider the symptoms of depression in relation to your child's gender. You may be less likely to notice that your little girl is quiet and withdrawn. It's simply more socially acceptable for a girl to behave in this manner than it is for a boy to appear docile and passive. As a result, girls tend to suffer from depression in silence more often than boys.

• **What is your child's age?** What is alarming at one age may be perfectly normal at another stage of development. Age-specific signs that may indicate depression include:

Infants
Failure to thrive and grow
Severe withdrawal
Excessive crying

Toddlers
Prolonged temper tantrums
Loss of interest in activities
Disturbed play

School-age children

Quiet, withdrawn behavior

Aggression/excessive anger

Physical complaints/frequent trips to the school nurse

Interest in morose or morbid subjects

Sudden, unexplained weight gain or loss

Inability to concentrate or perform schoolwork

Adolescents

Drug and/or alcohol use

Excessive crying

Loss of interest in family

School failure/truancy

Antisocial behavior

Increased fatigue

• **Has your child suffered a loss?** Dr. Mary Jane Sale says that when she is evaluating for depression, she always asks about a loss that the child may have experienced. The loss might be as obvious as the death of a family member or as subtle as the loss of security when a favorite toy or blanket is taken away.

• **What is your child's style of play?** A depressed child's style of play will often be developmentally below age level. Dr. Cynthia Pfeffer (1983) has observed that themes of play which are common among depressed kids include loss and retrieval, rescue, and fantasies about superheros. She also notes that these children are inclined to use their toys and their bodies in a reckless manner, such as throwing, jumping, performing dangerous stunts on their bikes, and pretending to fly.

Nicholas has a fascination with guns, knives, handcuffs, weapons of any form. At age eight he would play guillotine— pretending to whack off the heads of his toy Teenage Mutant Ninja Turtles®. He can fashion a perfect noose from the belt of a bathrobe. Last year he bought a hand grenade with his birthday money; this year he asked for a Samurai sword. What's next? A bazooka on his Christmas list.

Yet, this is the child who loves to visit the pet store so he can hold the puppies. The one who will carry a spider outside so I won't suck it up in the vacuum cleaner. And the same child who cuddled and rocked a friend's sick baby for an hour. I can't help but wonder what kind of scary world he lives in— this gentle Dragon who's armed to the teeth.

Depression Checklist

The following checklist will help you assess and document your child's feelings and behavior. This information will provide your physician or therapist with a fairly good picture of your child's emotional state.

Instructions: Make a copy of this checklist. Be as objective and thorough as possible. Use additional paper if you need more space to share your observations or give examples.

SIGNS OF POSSIBLE DEPRESSION (BASED ON YOUR OBSERVATIONS OF YOUR CHILD)	CHECK ALL THAT APPLY	DESCRIPTION: (HOW LONG? HOW OFTEN? GIVE EXAMPLES)
FEELINGS: Does your child express the following feelings?		
• Sadness		
• Emptiness		
• Hopelessness		
• Guilt		
• Worthlessness		
• Failure to enjoy everyday pleasures		
THINKING: Is your child having difficulty:		
• Concentrating		
• Making decisions		
• Completing school work		
• Maintaining grades		

SIGNS OF POSSIBLE DEPRESSION (BASED ON YOUR OBSERVATIONS OF YOUR CHILD)	CHECK ALL THAT APPLY	DESCRIPTION: (HOW LONG? HOW OFTEN? GIVE EXAMPLES)
PHYSICAL PROBLEMS: Does your child complain of:		
• Headaches		
• Stomachaches		
• Joint or backaches		
• Lack of energy, tired all the time		
• Sleeping problems (difficulty falling or staying asleep, or sleeping too much)		
• Weight or appetite changes (significant gain or loss)		
BEHAVIORAL PROBLEMS: Is your child:		
• Restless		
• Irritable		
• Not wanting to go to school		
• Wanting to be alone most of the time		
• Having difficulty getting along with others		
• Cutting classes or skipping school		
• Dropping out of sports, hobbies or activities		

SIGNS OF POSSIBLE DEPRESSION (BASED ON YOUR OBSERVATIONS OF YOUR CHILD)	CHECK ALL THAT APPLY	DESCRIPTION: (HOW LONG? HOW OFTEN? GIVE EXAMPLES)
• Drinking or using drugs		
SUICIDE RISK: Does your child talk or think about:		
• Suicide		
• Death		
• Other morbid subjects		

CHAPTER FIVE

WHAT ARE THE CAUSES OF DEPRESSION?

It's natural for both parents and children to seek a cause or reason for depression.

I have found that parents have lots of creative ways of assuming responsibility for their child's problems. They will assign blame to their lack of parenting skills or their demanding careers, their style of discipline or their own faulty upbringing. As a parent I have certainly wondered, if I had only done this or that differently, would my son be emotionally healthy and happy? By the same token, children may want to know why they feel lousy all the time. And if no credible answer is given, they are likely to assume it's just because they are "bad."

It's helpful for both parents and kids to understand the various elements that are associated with clinical depression. While the experts cannot offer a definitive cause, there does seem to be agreement that a variety of factors are involved in depression, including genetic, physical, psychological, and environmental.

Genetics: Climb Your Family Tree

There is clear evidence that depression runs in families. It may be in your genes.

One study revealed that a child who has one depressed parent stands a 30 percent chance of developing some form of depression during his or her lifetime. When both parents are depressed, the chance jumps to 70 percent. The National Institute for Mental Health - Yale Family Study reported that children between the ages of 6 and 17 who have depressed parents are two to three times more likely to develop a major depression than children whose parents are not depressed.

While a specific gene for depression has not yet been uncovered, studies of twins provide convincing evidence of a genetic link. If one identical twin has a depressive disorder, there is a 70 to 80 percent likelihood the other twin will also be afflicted. Among fraternal twins, as with other siblings, the risk is only about 25 percent. Identical twins reared apart are more likely to share a depressive disorder than fraternal twins who are reared together.

But depression is not passed along from parent to child in the same manner as eye color or height. Rather, children appear to inherit a predisposition to depression. This has sometimes been referred to as "genetic loading." A child with this vulnerability, when exposed to a major change, stress, loss or disappointment in life, is likely to experience a depressive illness.

When it comes to the question of nature vs. nurture, there's no clear winner. But we do know that nature plays a significant role in the development of depression.

Physical: The Mind and Body Connection

More than 30 years ago, physicians observed that certain medications had mood-altering effects. The blood pressure drug reserpine tended to cause depression, while isoniazid, used to treat tuberculosis, produced euphoria in some patients. These observations led to the realization that depressive disorders could be the result of a biochemical disturbance which might respond to treatment with drugs. Numerous laboratory and clinical studies followed—revolutionizing the treatment of mental illness.

Here is a simplified explanation of this process—one that even I can understand. (And bear in mind, I am one of those people who took the absolute minimum number of science credits to graduate from college.)

The brain uses "biochemical messengers" called neurotransmitters to process information. Electrical signals are transmitted from one neuron (nerve cell) to the next across synapses (the tiny gap between neurons) by neutotransmitters. This chemical signaling sets into motion the complex neural interactions that affect our thoughts, feelings, and behaviors. Different neurotransmitters have different jobs. Those responsible for regulating emotions are serotonin, dopamine, and norepinephrine. Various antidepressant drugs have been found to be effective in regulating the levels of neurotransmitters, and thereby in treating depressive disorders.

In another area of research that points to a biological cause for depression, it was found that patients with Cushing's disease suffer from depressed moods. These individuals have an excess of cortisol, a hormone associated with the body's ability to cope with stress. This observation led to measurements of cortisol in the blood and urine of other depressed patients. Approximately one-half had elevated levels while in a depressive episode, which dropped back to normal when they recovered.

Taking this one step further, researchers extended the knowledge that dexamethasone, which normally suppresses production of cortisol, does not do so in Cushing's patients. This same abnormal "nonsuppression" was found in significant number of depressed and bipolar patients. Using a dexamethasone suppression test (DST), it was found that about 70 percent of children with a major depression will have a positive DST.

Sleep studies are another promising area of biological investigation. Individuals with both unipolar and bipolar depression have different sleep patterns from those who do not have a depressive disorder. Those with mood disorders tend to experience the rapid eye movement (REM) phase of sleep associated with dreaming earlier. This is called "shortened REM latency." They have more eye movements during REM sleep, less deep or slow wave sleep, and a more difficult time staying asleep. As we know, common symptoms of depression are sleep-related problems and fatigue.

Unfortunately, the hormonal and sleep studies have not yet provided a definitive test for depression, nor have they pointed to a single cause. But they do provide substantial evidence of a biological basis for depression.

One may ask the proverbial chicken and egg question: Do these biochemical disturbances cause the depression, or are they a result of the depression? While that question remains unanswered, it is exciting to know that if researchers continue to unravel the biological links to depression, the next step will no doubt be more effective treatments and perhaps a prevention or cure.

Psychological: The Mind's Eye

There are a number of theories regarding the cause of depression that are based on one's psychological makeup. While these theories may be difficult to test or prove, in most cases they contain elements of what might be considered plain ol' common sense.

According to the psychodynamic theory (also called psychoanalytic theory), depression is the result of a real or imagined loss of a love object. A related theory is that depression is caused by the inability to achieve one's ego ideal. This perspective was promoted largely by Freud and Abraham.

A practical application of the psychodynamic theory is the definition of depression as "anger turned inward." Today, many clinicians believe that one important element of a depressed child's psychological make-up is anger that has been internalized and often finds inappropriate means of expression.

In the cognitive distortion model, depression is caused by a negative view of self, the world, and the future. Several studies do show that low self-esteem is present in depressed children (as in children with other psychiatric problems). And in one study, depressed children reported negative views of the future. No surprises here.

The learned helplessness model theorizes that depressed people come to believe that they have no control over their futures. Therefore, they feel helpless and give up on life. This helplessness is caused by motivational, cognitive, and emotional deficiencies.

The self-control model assumes that depressed people have deficits in self-reinforcement, self-monitoring, and self-evaluation. Most simply stated, they give credit to external forces for their successes and blame themselves for their failures.

In the social skill deficits model (also called the behavioral reinforcement model), people having inadequate social skills do not receive positive reinforcement from others, and this lack of positive reinforcement produces the depression.

Like the physical models, these psychological theories certainly raise the question of cause and effect.

Did the negative view of the world, the lowered self-esteem, the feelings of helplessness, the poor social skills, or the anger cause the depression or result from the depression? From a practical standpoint, I'm not sure it matters. What I did glean from this information is support for the notion that our cognitive, emotional, and physical components are truly intertwined.

Environmental: Impact of the World Around Us

I found it interesting to note that in the mid-1980s, there seemed to be a shift in the literature concerning childhood depression. Prior to that date, much of what was written focused on environmental causes. The blame was often laid at mother's feet—lack of warmth, lack of nurturing, lack of contact. (So where was father through all this?) The newer materials seem to give greater emphasis to biochemical and genetic causes.

Until researchers can point to a specific gene or produce a vaccine, perhaps we should maintain a balanced view of the causes of depression—a combination of physical, psychological, and environmental factors.

Let's face it, the world can be a pretty scary place. Children are exposed to trauma and violence, both in the media and in their day-to-day lives. Extended families are not as available as they used to be to provide a safety net. Drugs are filtering down to younger and younger children. Stresses of all forms are rampant.

The signs of stress in children identified by Dr. Antoinette Saunders and Bonnie Remsberg in their book, *The Stressproof Child* (1984), are, in actuality, the same as the signs of depression—somatic complaints, irritability, isolation, impulsivity, and problems with concentration, sleeping, and school performance.

Many life stressors that kids aged 6 to 13 identified in one study are external, environmental issues:

- Being afraid of strange animals, people and noises
- Pressure to perform academically
- Not being listened to
- Missing the family
- Threat of violence
- Being left alone
- Money worries
- Responsibilities
- Drugs
- Parents traveling
- Parents fighting

The numbers are staggering—depression among children is on the increase. So while the genetic and biological elements of depression cannot be overlooked, neither can the impact of a world that is spinning faster and faster, and through the eyes of a depressed child, maybe more than a little out of control.

Nicholas probably comes by his depression honestly. I've always known that my paternal grandmother and an aunt suffered from bipolar illness. And I've long suspected that my father had bouts of depression, too. But the most startling revelation was the day that my son's therapist slapped that label on me. He never actually used the word depression—but when he strongly suggested that I go on an antidepressant, I got the message.

Soon after Nicholas started seeing his present therapist, I made an appointment to talk about my son's progress. But three minutes into the conversation I found myself spewing like an oil gusher. I was carting around enough guilt to fill a steamer trunk. I just knew that all of my son's problems were my fault. Was it because I worked long hours? Or maybe the fact that I didn't breastfeed him as a baby. (I can't believe I actually said that.) I was speaking figuratively, but the good doctor flicked out the grain of sincerity from what I was saying. He told me I was "positively ruminating" and should consider trying some medication.

I thought he was kidding. I've always considered myself to be an enthusiastic, energetic person. I laugh a lot and I can make Pollyanna look like a pessimist.

But at that point, if the doctor would have told me that hopping on one foot in a circle and chanting a mantra in the middle of the shopping center would help my son, I'd probably have given it a try.

After three months of taking a fairly low dose of an antidepressant called Zoloft, I'm convinced this stuff should be added to the water supply. All joking aside, it was like getting glasses. I didn't realize how blind I was, until I could see. The particular strain of depression that I suffer from didn't affect my mood as much as it did my ability to concentrate. With medication, I was no longer dwelling on my son's problems. I became more emotionally available. I could think more clearly, and work became a pleasure once again—including writing. This book, as well as several others, are evidence of that.

In addition to inheriting a lousy gene pool, Nicholas has been dealt a number of other blows along the way. He struggles with a learning disability and a few neurologically crossed wires. This alone would be enough to produce a skewed view of the world. Add to that the deaths of his grandmother, grandfather, and great-grandmother, and the breakup of his parents' marriage—all within a three-year span. Who wouldn't be depressed? All things considered, I'd say Nicholas is a pretty buoyant child.

CHAPTER SIX

DIAGNOSIS: A FIRST STEP

Unfortunately, there is no simple test to accurately diagnose depression. A complete evaluation will typically involve:

- A physical examination
- Medical and psychiatric history
- A mental status examination

If you suspect that your child is suffering from depression, your family doctor or pediatrician is a good place to start. Make an appointment for an extended visit so you will have enough time to discuss all your concerns. Prepare in advance by completing the Depression Checklist on page 14.

Since there is a likelihood that you will need to share the same background information with several professionals, it is a good idea to make notes. That way you will not feel like a broken record, and you are less likely to forget critical facts with each repeated telling of your story. Here are the items that both medical doctors and mental health professionals may want to know:

- Any family history of depression, other emotional difficulties, or substance abuse

- Past episodes of depression, mental illness, or psychiatric treatment that your child has experienced

- Alcohol or drug use by your child

- The specific symptoms or problems you have observed, including physical, emotional, behavioral, and social

- When you first noticed a change in your child's behavior or mood

- Major losses, disappointments, or life changes that may impact your child's emotional state, such as a move, the death of a loved one, problems at school, divorce in the family, etc.

- Any prenatal or birth complications.

- Your child's medical history, including recent illnesses or injuries

- Medications that your child is now taking or has taken recently, including prescription and over-the-counter drugs

- Specific comments that your child has made about how he or she feels

- Questions you would like to ask the doctor

Your doctor will examine your child and may order some tests. The first step is to rule out any physical problems that may be causing him to appear depressed. I was surprised to learn the vast number of diseases and health problems that can mimic depression. Here are just some examples:

- Anemia
- Diabetes
- Infections
- Thyroid disorders
- Hypercalcemia (excessive calcium)
- Epilepsy
- Dermatomyositis (inflammatory disorder of muscles)
- Brain tumor
- Head injury
- Hypoglycemia
- Heart disease
- Parkinson's disease
- AIDS
- Drugs (prescription and illicit)
- Toxins (such as carbon monoxide)
- GI problems
- Multiple sclerosis
- Narcolepsy
- Renal diseases
- Sleep apnea
- Rheumatoid arthritis
- Vitamin deficiencies

Your physician will make a preliminary assessment of your child's mental status by evaluating his affect, thought processes, speaking patterns, and memory.

If no physical cause for the depression is found, your doctor may suggest a referral to a neurologist, psychiatrist, psychologist, or mental health clinic for additional testing and evaluation.

A neurological examination involves checking your child's reflexes, coordination, and balance. Your doctor may also order an electroencephalogram (EEG) or one of the brain scanning techniques to evaluate brain structure or functioning.

A psychiatrist or psychologist may use any or all of the following techniques to uncover the cause for a child's emotional distress:

- Interviewing the parents and child

- Reviewing the child's medical, psychiatric, and family history

- Conducting tests, including projective assessments like the Rorschach (commonly known as the "ink blot" test) and various other instruments like the Bellevue Index of Depression (BID), the Children's Behavioral Inventory (CBI), Childhood Depression Rating Scale-Revised (CDRS-R) and the Kiddie Schedule for Affective Disorder and Schizophrenia (K-SADS)

- Observing the child in free play or while interacting with the parents

- Asking the child to draw pictures

- Gathering input from the child's school and other sources

Once a thorough evaluation has been completed and a diagnosis of depression has been established, you can take the steps necessary to get help for your child. This is no time for home remedies and self-help. Depression is a real problem that requires professional help. The good news is that depression is one of the most treatable forms of mental illness, with 80 to 90 percent of all depressed patients having a positive response to treatment.

The process of having Nicholas tested—which stretched out for nearly seven years—was nothing short of torture. Unfortunately, many of the parents I interviewed had similar experiences. First, you have to pry yourself loose from denial, and admit that the teachers are not out to get your child and that something may indeed be wrong. While waiting for the results from a round of blood work early on, I can remember praying that all my child's problems would be attributed to an allergic reaction—you know, to something convenient like asparagus tips or a certain brand of laundry soap.

Then you bing-bong from doctor to doctor until, as one friend so aptly put it, you get the diagnosis you like. The hardest thing to deal with was the guilt. And no wonder. The first three professionals who evaluated Nicholas assured us that better parenting skills were all that was needed to set this child straight. I felt like a dog who kept getting swatted on the nose with a newspaper for peeing on the rug. Bad mother. Bad mother. I can actually remember wanting to inflict physical harm a time or two. But I figured that would be just the role modeling my already-aggressive son needed to send him on his way to Sing-Sing.

Helping Professionals

Choosing the right therapist for your child is a critical decision. There are various types of professionals that you might consider. Be sure to carefully check the credentials—including the educational background and licensure status—of any individual who may be involved in treating your child or family. Confidence and trust are at the heart of any therapeutic relationship.

Psychiatrists. Although any licensed physician can practice psychiatry, to be fully trained in this specialty requires completing a residency in psychiatry and passing an examination for board certification. Child psychiatry is a subspecialty that requires additional training and experience. A psychiatrist can diagnose and treat emotional problems, and prescribe medications.

Psychologists. In most states, a clinical psychologist has a Ph.D. and is licensed to diagnose and treat emotional disorders. A school psychologist may be involved in testing, evaluating, and treating your child, as well as assisting with educational planning and placement. Most states require a minimum of a Master's degree to be licensed in school psychology.

Social Workers. Be aware that the term "social worker" can be used loosely and may be applied to individuals with no particular training. A clinical social worker is trained in social work techniques including individual, family, and group therapy and case management and has a Master's degree (MSW) or a Doctorate (DSW). The initials LCSW after his or her name indicate that the social worker is licensed by the state licensing board.

Counselors. The term "counselor" may be applied to individuals with varied levels of training and expertise. This includes family counselors, pastoral or Christian counselors, and personal counselors.

Nurses. Registered nurses may receive special training in the treatment of emotional disorders. Psychiatric nurses typically have a Master's degree in this field. Nurse practitioners are able to prescribe medications in some states.

There are a variety of ways that you can locate a therapist:

- Contact the state licensure board for medicine, psychology, or social work to make sure the individual you are considering is properly licensed.

- Call your health insurance company to request a list of approved providers. Ask if you need pre-certification or a referral from your primary care physician.

- Ask your family physician, your child's guidance counselor or school psychologist, or local mental health association for suggestions.

• Call a physician referral service. These services are often sponsored by hospitals or medical societies.

• Talk with other parents who have children in treatment.

Of course, your child's needs should be the first consideration, but the reality of paying for treatment may also be an issue. If ability to pay is a problem, here are some tips that can help you secure the services you need in a cost-effective way:

• Contact your local community mental health center. Services are often provided on a sliding fee schedule according to your ability to pay.

• Hospitals and universities may offer therapy services through a clinic or research center.

• A psychiatrist will typically charge more than a psychologist, social worker, or counselor. You might consider using a psychiatrist for medication management and a less expensive professional for therapy.

Once you have identified a particular therapist, schedule an appointment for an initial interview. Ask the therapist about his or her training, background, philosophy, and treatment approach. Look for a therapist who has experience in treating children with problems similar to your child's.

Some therapists treat the patient individually, while others involve the parents and other members of the family in the process. You need to be comfortable with the level of family involvement that your therapist employs.

Whether or not you are actively involved in the therapy sessions, you will want to meet with the therapist periodically to discuss the therapy goals, your child's progress, and how you can best support your child at home.

If you are feeling uncomfortable about the diagnosis or treatment approach, don't hesitate to seek a second opinion. And, if you or your child have a difficult time relating to the therapist after a reasonable period of time, find a new therapist to whom you can relate.

I think we tried every variety of therapist available at least once. Most were caring and skilled. But we found at different points in time that a different type of therapist was called for.

Nicholas and I both had a wonderful therapeutic relationship with a female clinical psychologist for more than a year. We started seeing her when my husband and I were in the throes of separating with the goal of helping Nicholas adjust to the breakup of the family.

We survived that crisis. By then Nicholas was getting a little older—approaching those wonderful raging hormonal years of puberty. We all agreed that a male therapist might be more appropriate. This happened just when Nicholas was diagnosed with depression and we needed to shift to a psychiatrist for medication management. The solution was obvious—a male psychiatrist.

For me, trust, communication, and teamwork are essential. I have a need to take a very active role in Nicholas' therapy. (I'm sure there are times that his therapist would like a little less involvement on my part.) Although I must admit, it would be nice to turn my child over to his therapist and expect him to make him better and then send home when he's well. But that's not how it works. At least not on my planet. With a child like Nicholas, treatment has to be a long-term commitment—not a six-week emotional band-aid that the managed care companies are so fond of these days.

CHAPTER SEVEN

TREATMENT OPTIONS

In many cases, depressed children and their families can best be treated using a combination of approaches, which may include:

- Therapy
- Hospitalization
- Medication
- Educational assessment, planning, and placement

Types of Therapy

You and your child's therapist should work together to decide what type of treatment program would be best. This will depend upon your child's age, developmental level, emotional needs, and family situation.

• **Individual therapy.** Individual therapy involves an ongoing dialogue between the patient and therapist. For the treatment of mood disorders, Dr. Francis Mondimore (1990) suggests that the focus should be "encouragement, support, and education," rather than just self-understanding. While there are as many types of therapy as there are therapists, the following techniques have been found beneficial in treating depression:

    • Interpersonal therapy. Interpersonal therapy (IPT), developed by Dr. Gerald Klerman and Dr. Myrna Weissman, helps patients identify and deal with interpersonal problems that may have contributed to (or be caused by) depression. The goals of IPT are to improve self-esteem, social skills, and interpersonal effectiveness. IPT is short-term in nature.

    • Cognitive therapy. Cognitive therapy, developed by Dr. Aaron Beck, was specifically developed to treat depression. It is based on the premise that how you think affects how you feel. By correcting faulty thinking, a depressed person's negative view of himself, the world and the future will improve—relieving the depression in the process. As you might suspect, cognitive therapy for children has limitations. The child must be capable of "operational thinking" in order to benefit from this form of therapy.

• Behavioral therapy. Behavior therapy is based on the premise that the way you act affects the way you feel; that is, a depressed individual's behavior brings about negative consequences and deprives him of positive experiences.

This type of therapy may involve action-oriented assignments and skill development such as:

> Activity scheduling
> Assertiveness training
> Role playing
> Visualization
> Problem-solving
> Self-control training
> Relaxation techniques
> Time management
> Desensitization

Play therapy. Since play therapy takes advantage of nonverbal communication, it is useful for younger children and children who are developmentally delayed or noncommunicative. The therapist can learn a great deal about your child's feelings, relationships, self-concept, and view of the world by watching his manner of play. Play therapy also offers a safe environment for discharging aggression and stress, which may be particularly helpful for Dragons.

• **Group therapy.** Group therapy may be an appropriate option for a child who is feeling lonely and isolated. A group can provide a safe and supportive environment for a depressed child to express feelings and develop and practice social skills. It is also helpful for a child to realize that he or she is not the only child in the world who suffers from depression.

• **Family therapy.** A depressed child impacts everyone in the family, and parent or family therapy may be helpful. According to Drs. Rachel Klein and Cheryl Slomkowski (1993), "Providing professional help to parents and families does not imply that parental behavior is the root of the child's difficulties." A goal of involving other family members is to "enable them to become therapeutic agents for the child." A second goal is to reverse the negative effects of coping with a child with a psychiatric problem such as marital discord, divorce, and parental alcohol abuse. As mentioned previously, many depressed children have depressed parents. Treatment that involves the family can be significant in diagnosing and treating a parent who may be suffering from a depressive illness.

Just as the need for a particular kind of therapist changes over time, so does the need for a particular kind of therapy. In Nicholas' case, we opted for a combination of approaches. Individual therapy for Nicholas. Family therapy for all of us during our marital separation. Once we tried enrolling Nicholas in a group that was designed to bolster peer relationships. No success story here. Imagine ten ADHD boys in one room. I'm not sure if that therapist should be canonized or institutionalized.

Hospitalization

It is best to treat a child in the "least restrictive environment." Typically, this means in an outpatient setting. There may be some situations, however, where inpatient treatment is needed. This is usually limited to children who:

- Are clearly a danger to themselves or others
- Are medicating themselves with drugs or alcohol
- Need more intensive care than is possible on an outpatient basis
- Have a complicating medical condition in addition to the depression
- Have psychotic symptoms such as delusions or hallucinations

Whether or not to admit a child to a psychiatric hospital is a serious matter, one that you will want to discuss at length with your child's therapist. To help you explore this issue, Dr. Lawrence Kerns, in his book, *Helping Your Depressed Child: A Reassuring Guide to the Causes and Treatments of Childhood and Adolescent Depression* (1993), offers the following positive and negative aspects of inpatient care.

On the Downside:

- It sends a negative message to your child that he is totally out of control.

- Psychiatric hospitalization has a social stigma that your child will have to live with.

- Your child will experience a loss of freedom.

- The milieu—or environment—may not be good. Your child may be exposed to other very disturbed kids in this setting.

- The distance and separation may negatively impact the family.

- The expense is a very real concern, particularly with medical insurance covering less and less inpatient psychiatric care.

On the Upside:

- Medical supervision is available to ensure that your child's medication is providing the optimal therapeutic benefit.

• A hospital stay can offer a safe haven for a child who is seriously depressed, particularly one who is suicidal.

• The break may give needed relief—a respite—to other members of the family.

• Inpatient care gives an opportunity for more intensive therapy than can be delivered on an outpatient basis.

• The structured environment may provide your child with relief from the stresses of everyday living.

If it is determined that inpatient care is the best course of action for your child, Dr. Kerns offers the following steps to help you find the right hospital.

Discuss the selection of a facility with your child's therapist.

• Does this hospital specialize in treating children?

• Has your child's therapist admitted children to this hospital in the past? If so, how many? What were the outcomes for these patients?

Make necessary financial arrangements for admission.

• Will your medical insurance cover inpatient care at this facility? If so, how much?

• Is precertification (pre-approval from the insurance company) required prior to admission?

• Must you have a referral from your primary care physician?

• What is the hospital's payment policy relative to your co-pay, deductible, or uncovered expenses?

Tour the facility, and trust your instincts as you look around.

• How does the place feel? What is the general atmosphere? Is it relaxed and friendly or cold and institutional? Organized or chaotic?

• Does it appear to be clean, comfortable, and efficient?

• How do the staff members interact with the children? With one another?

• How do the kids look? Like zombies? Are they involved and active or sitting around looking bored?

Ask lots of questions.

• What are the goals of hospitalization? How will they be measured?

• What level of success has this hospital achieved with children who have been admitted? What is the average length of stay? How many children must be readmitted?

• Who will be involved with your child's treatment? What are their credentials? What are their functions?

• What type of family involvement is there? Will the parents and siblings participate in family therapy or counseling?

• How often will you receive progress reports? How will this information be conveyed?

• What is the academic program like?

• What will your child's schedule be each day? How much therapy will he receive in a day? In what other activities will your child be involved?

• What are the hospital's policies regarding visitation and phone calls?

• What will the hospital do to prepare the family prior to discharge? What follow-up services are available?

Medication

The antidepressant drugs used today are not really mood elevators. They do not make you happy or oblivious to the problems of living. Rather, they correct the biochemical functioning in the brain of a depressed individual. Medication can make your child more accessible. It can assist him in making a better social adjustment and allow him to benefit from therapy.

There are several main classifications of medication that may be prescribed for depression:

Tricyclics	
GENERIC NAMES	**TRADE NAMES**
imipramine	Tofranil, Imavate
amitriptyline	Elavil, Endep
nortriptyline	Aventyl, Pamelor
trimipramine	Surmontil
desipramine	Norpramin, Pertofran
protriptyline	Vivactil

In reviewing the literature, there appear to have been more studies related to the use of tricyclics with children, especially imipramine, than other classifications of antidepressants.

Lithium	
GENERIC NAMES	**TRADE NAMES**
lithium carbonate	Eskalith, Eskalith CR, Lithane, Lithobid, Lithotabs
lithium citrate	Cibalith-S

Lithium is technically not a drug, but rather an element. It is used to treat the mood swings associated with bipolar disorders.

Monoamine Oxidase (MAO) Inhibitors	
GENERIC NAMES	**TRADE NAMES**
tranylcypromine	Parnate
phenezine	Nardil
tranylcypromine sulfate	Parnate

MAO inhibitors can have a serious and even fatal effect on blood pressure and temperature when combined with certain foods, including aged cheese, yogurt, figs, chicken livers, and avocados, as well as some other drugs, such as cold medications. Your doctor will advise you about foods and drugs to avoid. These restrictions make MAO inhibitors somewhat problematic for use with children as it may be difficult to monitor everything they eat.

Selective Serotonin and Other Reuptake Inhibitors	
GENERIC NAMES	**TRADE NAMES**
fluoxetine	Prozac
citalopram	Celexa
maprotiline	Ludiomil
trazodone	Desyrel
paroxetine	Paxil
nefazodone HCL	Serzone
venlafaxine HCL	Effexor
sertraline HCl	Zoloft
sluvoxamine	Luvox
bupropion	Wellbutrin

The newest forms of antidepressants, including serotonin and other reuptake inhibitors, tend to have fewer side effects according to Jennifer Curry, PharmD. Bela Sood, M.D., Medical College of Virginia, notes that these drugs are safer should a patient overdose, and they have few cardio-toxic effects.

Patients respond differently to different medications; therefore, your doctor may need to try several medications or adjust the dosage level until arriving at the treatment that is most effective for your child. You are not likely to see an immediate benefit from medication. Some medications take several weeks to even begin having an impact. A minimum recommended trial for a medication is eight weeks after a therapeutic dosage level has been achieved. Others may notice an improvement before the patient himself does. Your child's sleep and appetite problems are likely to improve first. Next, he may regain some interest in friends and activities. Then, he may actually notice feeling better.

If your child has been diagnosed with both depression and ADD-ADHD, your doctor may prescribe an antidepressant instead of, or in addition to, Ritalin. It may be advisable to have a consultation with a psychopharmacologist, a specialist in managing medication for psychiatric disorders. This may be necessary when medication has not been effective, when an antidepressant is being combined with other medication, or when the child has a secondary medical condition. You can discuss this issue with your child's psychiatrist, pediatrician, or family physician.

Like all medications, antidepressants have a risk of side effects; therefore, your physician will monitor your child carefully. This is especially important during the first few months when serious problems are most likely to occur. Common side effects associated with antidepressants include:

- Dry mouth
- Constipation
- Problems urinating
- Blurred vision
- Dizziness
- Drowsiness

- Headaches
- Nausea
- Nervousness, jitters
- Insomnia
- Agitation
- Sexual problems
- Lightheadedness on getting up quickly
- Weight loss or gain
- Skin rashes
- Sweating
- Sun sensitivity

Many of these unpleasant reactions disappear after a week or two, once the body has had a chance to adjust. However, it is important to discuss possible side effects with your doctor. That way you will know in advance which are merely a nuisance, and which should be reported immediately. Abrupt discontinuation of an antidepressant can cause withdrawal symptoms such as anxiety, restlessness, and severe depression.

It's interesting to note that severity may be one of the factors used to determine which therapy is most effective. According to Dr. Irene Elkin (1990), the most severely depressed patients—those with the greatest functional problems—did better with medication, with less benefit resulting from psychotherapy. Less-depressed patients seemed to respond to any treatment regime.

Nicholas was about seven when he started taking Ritalin. Initially, I was dead-set against it. I thought we'd be drugging our child—setting him up for a life of dependency and addiction. I got over that. He was hard to handle at home, totally out of control at school. The final straw was being suspended from Sunday school.

The antidepressant didn't come for three more years. I was terrified when I found out that Prozac was the drug of choice. The media hype was pretty intense at that time. I read the books for and against. I talked to our family doctor and Nicholas' therapist. I spoke with psychiatric nurses and to parents whose kids were taking antidepressants. I looked up Prozac in the Physicians' Desk Reference. I'll never do that again. After reading that book, I'd be afraid to take an aspirin.

After one year on both medications, it seems that the Ritalin is really the most influential in keeping Nicholas' behavior in check. We've tried to reduce it three times, each attempt resulting in a rash of complaints from school. Nicholas will immediately start to fall down academically, and his relationships with other kids take a nose dive.

The only problem Nicholas has with his medication is some difficulty getting to sleep. There are nights that he is totally wired—then he'll wake up at 5:45 a.m. That's fine for a weekday, but on a Saturday morning that's what I call a serious side effect.

Educational Assessment, Planning, and Placement

The school system can be a valuable resource for testing and evaluation as well as educational planning and special services for your child.

Winifred Anderson's book, *Finding Help-Finding Hope: A Guidebook to School Services for Families With a Child Who Has Emotional, Behavioral or Mental Disorders* (1994), provides an excellent, comprehensive guide through the educational maze. In summary, these are the steps you will typically be required to take to secure special education services:

Referral

If you have concerns about your child's emotional condition, learning, or behavior, you may need to make a referral for evaluation and special educational services. This typically involves:

- Meeting with your child's teacher to discuss your concerns

- Contacting the principal or special education director to request a referral form for an assessment or meeting with the child study team or screening committee

- Gathering all the information you can to support your position that your child should be considered for special educational services. This should include test results, reports from your child's therapist, and documentation from any individual who has recently worked with your child

- Asking to attend the meeting at which your child will be discussed

The child study team will make recommendations for further evaluation or special support services. These recommendations will be presented to you in writing.

Evaluation

In order to determine if your child is eligible for special education services, the child study committee may recommend testing and evaluation. The evaluation will be conducted by a multidisciplinary team, which may include teachers, school psychologists, social workers, doctors, nurses, physical therapists, occupational therapists, speech therapists, and any other specialists needed to fully assess your child's needs. Your child may be evaluated educationally, psychologically, psychiatrically, and neurologically, if all these are indicated.

Before your child can be evaluated, you must give your consent. The school is required to tell you the purpose of the evaluation and the nature of the tests to be used. The evaluation process may involve any of the following components:

- Interviewing the parents and child

- Observing the child in the classroom setting

- Reviewing school records

- Evaluating medical history and any existing physical problems

- Conducting individual tests

- Reviewing records from other agencies or professionals involved with your child—with your written consent

When the evaluation is complete, you may request copies of the written reports, and you may meet with the evaluators to review the findings and ask questions. The evaluation results will be entered into your child's confidential file and may only be accessed by school staff who work with your child, unless you give written permission for a release of information.

If you do not agree with the evaluation, or feel the testing was incomplete, incorrect, or unfair, you may request an independent educational evaluation. The school system will be required to pay for this second opinion.

Individualized Educational Plan

Based upon the results of the assessment, an Individualized Educational Plan (IEP) will be developed for your child. Services such as speech, language, occupational and physical therapy, and special educational services or placement can be arranged as needed. You must approve your child's IEP, and due process rights are guaranteed, entitling you to an impartial hearing regarding any part of the plan.

The IEP must be reviewed and revised once a year. At least once every three years, every child who is receiving special education services must be reevaluated to determine whether the services are appropriate, and if the child is making progress.

The Law Is on Your Side

There are laws that protect your child's rights to school services. The four most significant laws that you should be aware of are:

• **The Individuals with Disabilities Act (IDEA)** is a comprehensive education law that guarantees all children with disabilities a free, appropriate, public education.

• **Section 504 of the Rehabilitation Act** prohibits discrimination by any agency that receives Federal funds against any individual on the basis of disability, including mental health problems.

• **The Americans with Disabilities Act (ADA)** is an antidiscrimination law that protects the civil rights of individuals with disabilities. This is similar to the protection against discrimination on the basis of race, gender, national origin, or religion.

• **The Family Educational Rights and Privacy Act (FERPA),** also called the Buckley Amendment, guarantees the privacy of school records. It also ensures the parent's right to see, review, and, if necessary, amend the child's school records.

The school system is obligated to provide an appropriate education for your child in the "least restrictive environment." For some children, this may mean remaining in the classroom, while seeing the school psychologist or counselor on a regular basis. For another child, special placement in the school system may be warranted. In extreme cases, services at a private school or treatment facility may be needed to meet a child's needs.

We've been fortunate to be able to send Nicholas to private school. Since he was two-and-a-half, he has attended the local Montessori School, where his father is a teacher. But even in the best of schools, all is not perfect.

Nicholas' emotional problems first became apparent in the structure of the school setting. From the beginning, this was no typical preschooler. He gave a whole new meaning to "the terrible twos." Sitting still for story time was impossible. He was strong-willed and didn't have a clue as to why anyone would even expect him to do what he was asked. His first teacher—a real sweetie with kids—noticed that he would recoil whenever she touched him. He was like a animal caught in the headlights: huge eyes, filled with terror.

Second year. This poor child had the teacher-from-hell. He spent at least half of every day in the time-out chair and hated school. No wonder. I observed his class for an hour and kept thinking, "If she's this cold to the kids when a parent is in the room, what is she like when she's alone with them?" Then she actually pinched my child when he didn't spring out of his chair on command. That did it.

The next day, Nicholas was moved to another room. It was either that, or we would have moved him to another school. In fact, for several months he was placed in his father's class. This proved to be a good move, and Nicholas started to enjoy school for the first time.

The last few years have been better. The Montessori School provides a very protective environment. His teachers are flexible and incredibly tolerant. I can't even imagine this child making it in a public school, where 32 kids per class is the norm. Still, three times a year, when it's time for parent-teacher conferences, I can feel my heart palpitating. The standardized test scores keep saying he's pretty much on par academically. But I know he really struggles at school. Homework is a challenge. One day he can do a lesson, the next day it's lost. As for his problems getting along with peers—that's a constant.

But every once in a while there's a breakthrough. Like this year, when Nicholas has one-to-one math instruction. He absolutely struts every time he brings home a pop quiz marked with a huge red "A." I know not everyone is lucky enough to be able to send their child to a private school. In our case, I would give up eating to pay the tuition if that was necessary. There's no sense saving money for college if he can't make it through sixth grade.

CHAPTER EIGHT

PARENT'S SURVIVAL GUIDE:
WHAT CAN YOU DO TO HELP YOUR CHILD?

Personally, I feel better when I can do something—that is, take action to tackle a problem. It sure beats sitting around whining.

Over the course of the past eight years, I think I tried everything at least once to help my son Nicholas. Some strategies were successful; most were short-lived. What works for one child may have no bearing on another. The following pages contain a number of ideas that are based on my personal experience, the experiences of other parents, and suggestions from various mental health professionals.

You know your child and your family situation. So pick a tactic and give it a try for a reasonable period of time. If nothing else, maybe you'll feel better for the effort.

Get in Touch with Your Own Feelings

Parenting is a tough job under the best of circumstances. There are a broad range of emotions that parents may feel when their children are suffering from depression. First, be honest with yourself. Then seek help to sort out any feelings that may not be supportive of your child's development. Your ability to accept your child—or your failure to do so—can have a profound impact on his already damaged self-esteem. And we all know that kids have a sixth sense about these things. They can sniff out a fake reaction faster than a bloodhound.

These are just some of the difficult emotions that you may experience. I certainly felt all of them at one time or another.

- **Guilt.** I must have asked myself a million times, "What did I do to cause this?" In fact, it was this very question that prompted Nicholas's therapist to tell me that I was "ruminating" and wasting a lot of energy. Depression is a complicated illness that cannot be attributed to any one incident in your child's life. And you certainly cannot be held accountable for your defective genes. Blame your ancestors for that one. So get off the guilt trip and start focusing on solutions. Put all that energy to productive use.

- **Fear.** What will happen to my child in the future? How will we make it though all the trials and tribulations of the teen years? Will my child be able to lead a happy, productive life or will this depressive state continue? Fretting about your 10-year-old's prospects for college admission or career success may be pressure that she doesn't need to bear. Just take it one day at a time.

• **Anger.** Sometimes you'll be mad at the world. Why did this happen to my child? Why did this happen to me? (I've been known to slide into this line of thinking while I'm listening to my friends talk about little Billy's selection for the gifted class or Suzy's overflowing social calendar.) Then there are times you may be aggravated with your child himself—especially when he goes into a major oppositional jag. Honest expression of emotion is perfectly OK. In fact, it is good to model appropriate ways of expressing anger for your child. Dr. Thomas Gordon, founder of Parent Effectiveness Training (PET), suggests using an "I" message rather than a "You" message. Here is an example: "I really don't like to come home from work and find the sink full of dirty dishes." It sure beats saying, "You're so lazy. Can't you ever clean up after yourself?"

• **Embarrassment.** There are few things that are more humiliating than being in the middle of a restaurant or department store and having your child throw a fit. I've been there. Evonne Weinhaus and Karen Friedman, in their book, *Stop Struggling with Your Child* (1991), offer a wonderful bit of advice: Don't judge your success as a parent by your child's response to any situation. Rather, judge your success based on your own reaction. (And if that fails, pretend you're the babysitter.)

• **Disappointment.** We all want the best for our children—an excellent education, a good career, a happy life. It's scary to think that your child's condition may interfere with any or all of your visions for the future. Your dreams and expectations may not be your child's. Focus on helping your child feel good about himself, and the rest will take care of itself.

• **Hopelessness.** At times it seems difficult to envision your family situation ever improving, and you might have an overwhelming sense of despair and hopelessness. If you give up on your child, he will give up on himself. But remember, depression is highly responsive to treatment. Many famous and accomplished people—Patty Duke, just to name one—have struggled with depression and won. As an added note, be aware that feelings of hopelessness just might be a reflection of your own depression, which you are attributing to your child's problems and behavior.

Look in the Mirror

Evaluate your own emotional status. Depressed parents have depressed kids. In addition to the genetic implications, depressed parents are depressed role models. And they may be emotionally unavailable to their children. It's not hard to see where Nicholas's depression comes from. We have a family history that can be traced back at least three generations, and who knows how long before that. Seeking treatment for myself was perhaps the most therapeutic step I could have taken to help my son.

Don't Lose Sight of the Child

I love my son dearly, but I must admit there are times when he is tough to like. Dragons are oppositional, negative, and angry. Turtles may be unresponsive and flat. Not exactly cuddly puppies in either case.

But don't forget that on the inside, every depressed child—no matter how prickly or off-putting their behavior may be—is a deeply saddened and distressed boy or girl. A child crying for warmth and love, attention, and reassurance. Be tender. Give hugs for no reason. Tell your child you love him as often as you can.

Be Honest

One day my son was watching television and an ad for a local psychiatric hospital came on the air. The ad ticked off six or eight signs of depression. My son looked me straight in the eye and said, "That's just how I feel. Does that mean I'm depressed?" This occurred several months before he was tested and "officially" diagnosed.

It was really tempting to say, "No honey, you're just a little down right now, but you'll be fine." Like all moms, I wanted to be reassuring: kiss it and make it all better.

But, I resisted the cover-up and responded, "You know, son, you just might be. Let's share your feelings with your therapist. I think it will help her to help you."

Your child knows he feels awful. You cannot make those bad feelings go away by ignoring his plea for help or discounting his pain. By validating your child's emotions, even the unpleasant ones, you will encourage him to open up and share what's really inside.

Be Empathic

When I was an undergraduate, my Psych 101 professor defined empathy as "your pain in my heart." Get in touch with your child's feelings. When your kid's sulking and slinking around or acting out, ask what she needs at that very moment. Try to put yourself in your child's place. See the world through her eyes.

Be an Active Listener

Busy moms and dads are usually half-hearted listeners. Take a few minutes to really connect with your child. Active listening has the following components:

- Eye contact. Look at your child, not the TV or morning newspaper.

- Attentive body language. Lean toward your child. Nod your head to let your child know you heard what is being said. Sit very close to your child when you are talking. You're less likely to be distracted.

- Be quiet. Close your mouth and resist the temptation to offer an immediate solution or the ever popular "I've-tried-to-tell-you this before" lecture. Dr. Antoinette Saunders and Bonnie Remsberg in their book, *The Stressproof Child* (1984), suggest that you ask your child in advance what topics she would like to talk about, and how she would like you to respond. Your child may indeed be looking for a suggestion. But more likely, she is seeking a sounding board or a partner with whom to commiserate. Most of all, she wants to know that you care about whatever is important to her.

- Verbal following. Make little "I'm listening" sounds—like "Oh," "Really," "Hum." Or restate what you heard your child say, like, "It made you feel sad when Casey asked Robert to the game instead of you." (Simply paraphrase what you heard, don't get into fancy interpretations.) This ensures the child that you are tuned in, and it gives him a chance to correct any miscommunication.

- Make sharing time a priority. Set aside time to talk with your child on a regular basis. It may only be 15 minutes every Saturday morning. But make sure that time is sacred. Even if your child isn't in the mood to talk every time, let him know that this time is reserved just for him.

Help Your Child Express Emotions

Provide your child with an emotionally expressive environment by:

- Teaching her a "feelings vocabulary." Sometimes kids don't express their feelings because they simply don't have the proper words to do so. There are wonderful books, posters, and games that can help your child understand and label her feelings.

- Being a positive role model. Show your child healthy ways to express emotions of all kinds, how to show affection and how to appropriately handle anger and frustration. Let your child know that all emotions are OK. It's the manner of expression that is acceptable or not.

Cut Your Losses

Loss and grief are common elements of depression. The loss may be something that's very apparent, like the death of a beloved grandparent or family pet. Or it may be less obvious, such as the loss of self-esteem your daughter may experience when she is assigned to the blue reading group rather than the red group.

Just because your child is smiling on the outside, it doesn't mean she's not suffering on the inside. You can help your child through the grieving process by:

- Letting your child know that losing something or someone special hurts. Give her "permission" to grieve.

- Encouraging your child to talk about her full range of feelings —joy, anger, sadness, denial, guilt, and fear.

- Holding onto the good feelings. When my father died, I gave Nicholas a collection of memorabilia—my father's military medals, high school class ring, photographs, and the American flag that was presented at his funeral. With these things, Nicholas created a "memory box" to help him capture all the warm and loving feelings he had for his grandfather.

Another healthy technique for dealing with the loss of a loved one is to take on a positive characteristic of that individual. Let's say a close friend or relative dies or moves away. Or perhaps your child is feeling the loss of a favorite teacher when it's time to move on to the next grade level. In these cases, you can help by asking your child what he liked or admired most about this person. Then you can encourage him to adopt that trait. Your child can keep the memory alive by being as nice as Grandpa, as confident as Billy, or as courageous as Mr. Jones.

- Letting go. My son was deeply saddened when he didn't make the travel soccer team. In this case, it made sense to help him let go of those feelings and move on. Rather than dwelling on the loss, I encouraged him to focus his energies on a brand new activity, which turned out to be archery. While it was important to recognize the pain Nicholas had experienced, it was equally important to help him learn a coping mechanism and regain his sense of control.

Boost Your Child's Self-Esteem

You can help boost your child's poor self-image by zeroing in on his positive attributes and ignoring as many negative things as you can. Instead of praising the child for accomplishments and achievements, you might try to focus on:

- Your child's intrinsic goodness. Your child's goodness comes from within. Reinforce attributes of caring, gentleness, patience, and sensitivity in your Dragon and assertiveness, socialization, and emotional expression in your Turtle. The concept of "unconditional love" was never more essential than for supporting a depressed child. Like Mr. Rogers says in his trademark line, "I like you just the way you are."

• **Your child's effort.** Not trying and giving up are common ailments of kids who are feeling down in general—and down on themselves in particular. Praise your child for trying something new or sticking with a tough assignment, regardless of the outcome.

• **Your child's intentions.** One night at 1 a.m., I was totally exasperated to find my son running around the house, hauling everything imaginable out of the hall closet. At first he said he was looking for a stuffed toy. Finally he admitted that "Fluffy" had gotten loose and was hiding somewhere in the house. My reply: "What exactly is 'Fluffy?'" It seems that Fluffy was a tiny duckling that my son valiantly "rescued" from the pond near our house and brought home so it wouldn't be lonely and scared.

As upset as I was that my son had jumped into the pond—which was a definite no-no in our house—I told him how touched I was by his concern for this cute little critter. And he was a real cutie.

Catch Your Child in the Act of Being Good

Most simply stated, many depressed kids think they are bad. So take every opportunity to catch your child in the act of being good. No matter how small the deed, turn it into a compliment. Dr. Mary Jane Sale suggests that you pay special attention to behaviors that involve relating to others in a positive way, such as:

• Grandpa really appreciated the big hug you gave him today.
• I liked the way you held the door open for the lady in the store.
• That was very kind of you to share your candy with Nathan.
• It was so nice to see you hold the puppy so gently today.

Tame the Dragon

Some kids, but especially Dragons, are masters of oppositional behavior. They love to engage in power struggles, and moms are an all-time favorite target. This is a case where an ounce of prevention may save you from a pounding headache. The following are a few tips to help you stay out of the war zone:

• **Be consistent.** Children feel most secure in an environment where the limits are clearly defined and consistently applied. Establish a routine and work within it. Make a rule and stick to it. State a consequence and enforce it.

• **Use natural consequences.** Your child is late for dinner for the fifth night in a row. You're tired. You're sick of being treated like a short-order cook. First you lecture him for 15 minutes about being inconsiderate. Next you punish him by taking away a privilege or grounding him the next day after school. Then you prepare his dinner—all the while continuing the verbal assault. Finally, you swear that this is the very last time you will ever prepare a second meal if he is late to dinner. Sound familiar?

The next time this scenario happens, allow "natural consequences" to prevail. If your child misses dinner, either he doesn't eat or he must prepare his own meal and clean up afterward. He made the choice to be late; now let him live with the consequences. This is a far less combative approach. It puts your child in control of the outcome and removes you from the role of "enforcer."

• **Take a break.** When you're feeling your blood pressure rise as a major confrontation starts to brew, remove yourself from the situation. Tell your child that you are feeling angry or frustrated, and you need some time to cool down. Leave the room. Read in the bathroom. Take a walk around the block. You and your child can't "go at it" if you get out of the ring.

• **Just say "Yes."** A wonderful strategy, found in Weinhaus and Friedman's book, *Stop Struggling with Your Child* (1991), demonstrates the power of a single word. Instead of saying "No," say "Yes." Here is how it works:

Don't say: "No, you may not have a cookie because we're going to eat dinner in 15 minutes."

Do say: "Yes, you may have a cookie—right after dinner."

At the mere mention of the word "No" your child may prepare for battle. When you say "Yes" there's nothing for your child to argue about.

Help Your Child Develop Social Skills

One of the most heartbreaking aspects of childhood depression is social withdrawal. I lost count of the number of times my son tearfully said, "I don't have any friends." This isolation can occur with Turtles as well as Dragons. Provide your child with as many social opportunities as possible.

I choose to coach my son's soccer team to make sure that he has a positive experience with this group of kids. You may not want to go to that extreme. But you can arrange play days, outings, and sleepovers. Stock your freezer with popsicles, fill your refrigerator with juice boxes, rent fun movies, and resort to other forms of bribery to make your house a fun destination for other kids.

Depressed kids seem to do best playing with gentle, passive children. Quiet kids won't overwhelm a Turtle, nor are they likely to butt heads with a Dragon. I also discovered that activities of a shorter duration tend to have more favorable outcomes than marathon get-togethers.

In addition to socializing one-on-one, being part of a group is an important element of social development. Organized sports teams, Scouts, or any type of club will fulfill your child's need to feel connected. Dr. Mary Jane Sale advises that kids who do not feel that they belong may be attracted to a gang. So you decide. Cub Scouts or the Blue Devils. YMCA basketball team or the Thugs.

Use Your "Parent Power"

• The power of touch. A warm, gentle touch can be a powerful form of communication. When your Dragon is out of control, use a secure hug to restrain him. And when your Turtle is feeling particularly vulnerable, a little squeeze can give her immediate support.

• The power of humor. Don't get so caught up in your child's emotional problems that you forget the importance of fun. There are times that a genuine smile or laugh can break the tension of the moment. This is a great way to model the use of humor as an effective means of dealing with frustration. One point of caution, however: while it's OK to poke a little fun at yourself, make sure that your child doesn't feel that you are laughing at her.

• The power of speaking softly. There may be times that it is best to approach your child in a gentle manner. A quiet, soft approach can be soothing to a Dragon and is less likely to intimidate a Turtle.

Don't forget the adage, "When you want to capture someone's attention, whisper." Whispering beats shouting nearly every time. And when you're in the presence of other people, it's a great way to get your child's attention and address a behavioral problem without embarrassing him in the process. Saving face is important to keep in mind if you are trying to bolster your child's self-esteem.

You Are What You Eat

Eating problems are common symptoms of mood disorders. A depressed child may not have much of an appetite, or she may seek comfort through food.

The relationship between a balanced diet and emotional well-being has been recognized for a number of years. The literature is sprinkled with articles on the consequences of inadequate nutrition—namely, social withdrawal, decreased concentration, sleep disturbances, irritability, apathy and, you guessed it, depression.

As a parent, perhaps the best rules to follow regarding your child's nutrition are driven by common sense. Eileen Stellefson, RD, Nutrition Specialist for the Eating Disorders Program at the Medical University of South Carolina, offers the following guidelines:

- Do not classify food items as either "good" or "bad." This form of judgement contributes to power struggles and feelings of guilt.

- Provide three well-balanced meals a day.

- Allow sugar and fats, but not to excess or in place of a wholesome diet.

- Watch out for caffeine, sodium, and chemical additives, all of which tend to abound in kids' favorite snack foods. But don't be a fanatic—an occasional Twinkie never hurt anyone.

- Do not use food as a means of nurturing your child. Rather than rewarding your child with a cookie, give him a hug. Instead of a piece of cake, take a nice long walk together.

- Serve as a role model for good eating habits.

- Stock your refrigerator and cupboard with healthy, fun treats—like fresh fruit, yogurt, cereal bars, and fruit juice.

Most importantly, don't allow food to become one more source of stress in your child's life. Mealtime should be relaxed and enjoyable. This is a time for sharing the day's events, not battling over uneaten brussels sprouts.

Cultivate Your Child's Hobbies and Activities

Hobbies of all kinds can benefit a depressed child. Encourage those activities that your child enjoys—it might be anything from calligraphy to music, Civil War history to bird watching. Hobbies can provide a source of pleasure, which is particularly important for kids who don't seem to smile very often. They permit a child to experience a sense of mastery and accomplishment. And if you seek out groups, clubs, or other children with similar interests, you can convert a solitary activity into a social opportunity.

Dr. Gerardo Crichigno suggests that some children can turn their interests into volunteer activities—another terrific way to enhance self-esteem and encourage socialization.

Just Do It

Provide your child with plenty of opportunities for physical exercise. Physical exertion releases natural endorphins, which have an emotionally uplifting effect. (Long-distance runners experience a kind of "high" from this effect.)

Tae Kwon Do is a great form of exercise for any depressed child. A Turtle will gain confidence.

A Dragon will learn self-control and discipline, not to mention blow off a lot of steam in the process. Just make sure the school's philosophy is centered on character development rather than inflicting bodily harm.

Soccer is another terrific physical activity. This is one sport that children of any age, size, or physique can play. And there are plenty of recreation leagues that focus on skill development, fitness, and sportsmanship, rather than blood and guts competition. Soccer also emphasizes teamwork and provides lots of opportunity for socialization. Be sure to discuss your child's emotional status with the coaches in advance so they can provide an extra measure of support.

Perhaps your child is not particularly athletic. In this case, your insistence that he play a team sport can lead to one more "failure." Help your child find a physical activity that is noncompetitive, like power walking, rollerblading, or horseback riding. One parent discovered that weight lifting was the perfect sport for her teenage son. He could see the results of his efforts—while he was building muscle, he was building self-esteem.

When your child is feeling stressed or anxious, suggest a five-minute "power break." Jumping rope, running around the block or, my son's favorite, bouncing on my mini-trampoline, can provide a needed bit of relief, especially during homework time.

Become an Expert

When my child was first diagnosed with depression, I had a difficult time finding books on the subject. But with a little digging, I uncovered a wealth of valuable information. The more I learned, the more I felt I could support and help him. You will find a Resource Guide in the back of this book. It lists books, associations, and other sources of information to help your child and yourself. Five resources that I found to be particularly helpful were:

- *Parent Effectiveness Training (PET)* by Dr. Thomas Gordon

- *Stressproof your Child* by Dr. Antoinette Saunders and Bonnie Remsberg

- *Stop Struggling With Your Child* by Evonne Weinhaus and Karen Friedman

- *The Optimistic Child: A Revolutionary Program that Safeguards Children Against Depression and Builds Lifelong Resilience* by Dr. Martin Seligman, Karen Reivich, Lisa Jaycox, and Jane Gillham

- *Helping Your Depressed Child: A Reassuring Guide to the Causes and Treatments of Childhood and Adolescent Depression* by Dr. Lawrence Kerns with Adrienne B. Liebermann

While the first three do not focus on childhood depression, they all contain valuable and practical suggestions for you to try.

Advocate for Your Child in School

Be involved with your child's school. Get to know the teachers, counselors, school psychologists, and social workers. Be sure they understand the nature of your child's depression and needs. Be available, and play an active role in planning, implementing, and evaluating your child's IEP.

It may be helpful to arrange a conference between your child's therapist and the various professionals at the school. This will ensure that everyone who is involved with your child is working toward the same goals and applying the same strategies.

A few parents whom I interviewed discovered that the schools were not anxious to formally label their children depressed, emotionally disturbed, or learning disabled. Such a diagnosis means that the school system must provide—and pay for—special educational services. I was pleased to learn, however, that most parents had very positive experiences with their school systems. They found the professional staff to be knowledgeable and genuinely interested in meeting their child's needs.

Maintain Your Own Support System

You can join an organized support group or tap into your informal network of friends and family. I have several friends who also have children with ADHD or emotional problems. They are truly sensitive to how I feel. And when we spend time together with the kids, they understand why my son may be dangling from the light fixture or sulking in the bathroom.

Get a Life

Don't center your entire existence around your child's emotional difficulties. Take time for yourself. Cultivate your own interests and friendships. A comment by Dr. Thomas Gordon speaks to this very issue. He says, "A parent with a half-filled cup cannot give his child a drink."

Do things with your child. Enjoy activities with your family. Don't forego an outing because you're afraid your child may act out or somehow embarrass you. If the kid acts out, he acts out. Deal with it. But don't create a self-fulfilling prophecy. Make sure you give adequate attention and time to all the members of your family—especially your other children.

Trust Your Instincts

While professional input is important, you know your child better than anyone else. Don't underestimate your own ability to understand your son or daughter and to be genuinely therapeutic. Your love and support are without a doubt the most important elements in treating and caring for any depressed child.

Look for Positive Signs

Dr. Mary Jane Sale shared a wonderful yardstick by which to measure improvement. You will know your child is making progress when her periods of anger, withdrawal, or noncompliance occur with:

- Less frequency.

- Less intensity.

- Less duration.

- Greater stimulus. (In other words, your child is able to cope better with the little frustrations—she only falls apart when something major happens.)

Don't look for perfection. Even the most well-adjusted child will have bad days. Don't overinterpret every little thing. Be aware of self-fulfilling prophecies. You child will know if you expect her to respond in a negative way, and she will live up to your expectations.

My son had a near brush with the law at age 10. In an effort to re-establish trust, I told him how lucky he was to have made his mistakes early on —like he's only entitled to one round. Since he learned a lesson from the experience, now he won't make those same bad choices when he is a teenager, when he would get into more serious trouble. It gave him a chance to save face and didn't set up the expectation that he would mess up again.

Pulling Together—Even When You're Apart

A key to helping a child cope with marital discord or the separation or divorce of his parents is to give him permission to love and have a close relationship with both his mother and his father.

Most simply stated, if you and your spouse have made the decision to end your marriage, don't drag your child into the middle of the battleground. Your child's self-image is, in large part, a reflection of his view of both parents. If Mom is a bad person, so am I. If Dad is a creep, I must be a creep, too.

So set aside your differences and make a firm commitment to put your child's needs first. Refrain from making negative comments about one another. Avoid blaming and finger-pointing. Provide your child with free access to the other parent. Try to be as consistent as possible in your styles of parenting. Make major decisions about your child as a team. Work together to support your child's therapy. In a word, be a good "co-parent."

The concept of co-parenting is not limited to parents who are living apart. It can also apply to families that are intact. Even moms and dads who are together can unknowingly pull and tug at their children.

A Special Word for Moms

Nicholas is one of those kids who will be calm and well-behaved with his father and an out-of-control maniac with me. It is incredibly frustrating.

One of the greatest gifts I ever received was a book written by Russell Barkley, Ph.D., entitled *Attention-Deficit Hyperactivity Disorder: A Handbook for Diagnosis and Treatment*. Dr. Barkley, one of the country's leading authorities on ADD-ADHD, published a study on the level of acting-out behavior by ADHD boys with their mothers as compared to their fathers. He found overwhelming evidence that ADHD boys are more likely to act out with Mom than with Dad. In interviews with various clinicians, there was unanimous agreement that this same finding holds true for depressed kids—in fact, all kids.

I'd like to share one paragraph from Dr. Barkley's book that I found particularly helpful:

> "I have encountered fathers who either do not believe that their children have any problems or refuse to admit that the problems are as serious as the mothers report them to be. In some cases, the fathers may believe that their wives are overly sensitive to what they themselves label as merely normal childhood exuberance in boys. In others, the fathers believe that their wives are simply too permissive and unwilling to discipline the children. This can sometimes lead to the insistence by the fathers that their wives, not their children, are in need of professional assistance...It's time for fathers and male professionals to realize that children, especially ADHD children, do show differences in the actual manner in which they respond to their mothers compared to their fathers. This does not necessarily implicate flaws in the mother's caretaking abilities or an excessive sensitivity to normal child behavior."

An Ounce of Prevention

As I was taking the final steps toward completing this book, I discovered an incredibly refreshing resource—*The Optimistic Child: A Revolutionary Program That Safeguards Children Against Depression & Builds Lifelong Resilience*.

The title says it all. Dr. Martin Seligman, one of the nation's leading experts in the field of childhood depression, and his colleagues at the University of Pennsylvania published the results of a long-term study on the prevention of depression. Yes, that's right—prevention. They actually talk about "psychologically immunizing" children against depression by teaching them to challenge their pessimistic thoughts and approach life with a sense of genuine optimism, self-esteem, and confidence.

CHAPTER NINE

WHAT ELSE DO YOU NEED TO KNOW?

Depression usually doesn't stand alone. There are other issues that you should be aware of in order to fully understand your child's needs. By being alert to the various risk factors and problems that may accompany depression, you can give your child the best possible chance for a successful outcome.

Depression and Social Relationships

Depressed children have problems with interpersonal relationships. They may have strained relationships with parents and teachers as well as difficulties making and keeping friends. Dr. Kevin Stark (1994) reports that many of these social problems are linked to the way that a depressed child thinks about social interactions. That is, the child expects to be rejected or have some other negative response when he enters a social situation. As a result, he is flooded with negative thoughts and reacts in an angry or withdrawn manner. This elicits a negative response from others, and the child's expectations are fulfilled. This same pattern is repeated again and again.

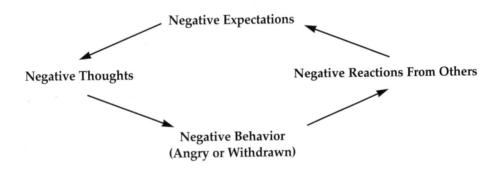

A significant aspect of therapy for depressed children is helping them to improve relationships with both peers and authority figures.

Depression and Eating Disorders

Starvation can have a pretty dramatic impact on one's emotional well-being and behavior. Here are some of the ways malnourishment can take its toll:

- Poor judgement
- Weakness
- Sleep disturbances
- Personality changes on psychological tests
- Social withdrawal
- Psychotic episodes
- Irritability
- Anger
- Anxiety
- Depression
- Apathy
- Decreased concentration
- Hyperacuity to noise and light

According to the National Association of Anorexia Nervosa and Associated Disorders, eating disorders affect eight million people in this country alone, many of them children who are much younger than one would expect. And as many as four out of five eating disorder patients will suffer from depression during their lifetimes.

Depression and Learning

Dr. Joaquim Puig-Antich (1983) reports that depression can result in impaired cognitive ability, poor concentration and, ultimately, damaged school performance. Depressed kids scored lower than nondepressed kids in reading, writing and math. As you might expect, the poor scholastic performance made these children feel worse about themselves, and the spiral continued to turn downward. He cautioned that, if left untreated, the effects of poor academic performance and its impact on self-esteem can continue into adulthood.

Depression and ADD-ADHD

Do ADD-ADHD kids suffer from depression more often than normal kids? The jury is still out. Some studies found a higher prevalence of depression among children with ADD-ADHD, while others did not.

According to Dr. Russell Barkley, "sad affect" in an ADD-ADHD child may be the result of school failure and lack of acceptance by peers. These children might appropriately be diagnosed as having an Adjustment Disorder with Depressed Mood. In cases where clinical depression and ADD-ADHD do occur together—called comorbidity—these disorders should be treated as separate and equally primary problems, rather than viewing one as secondary to the other.

Depression and Suicide

At 11:30 p.m. on August 2, 1994, my son, then 10 years of age, held a toy gun to his head and said, "If it was real, I'd use it." I believed him. It was the most terrifying moment of my life.

No doubt the most frightening ramification of depression is the risk of suicide—and it is a very real risk indeed.

Age has a marked impact on suicide risk. While younger children may have suicidal thoughts, kids over the age of 15 are more likely to actually attempt or commit the act. They are more capable of planning and carrying out a suicide, plus they are contending with all sorts of raging hormonal influences.

Suicide is the second leading cause of death among teens, with accidents being the number one. Yet, one has to wonder, how many deaths which are officially classified as accidents are really suicides, or at least related to a depressive state, particularly when drugs or alcohol are involved?

Among children between the ages of 5 and 15, suicide is the fifth leading cause of death. In 1992, there were 314 suicides among children in this age bracket in this country. And as unbelievable as it may seem, children as young as three or four have taken their own lives.

Gender also has a bearing. Among adolescents, girls are more likely to attempt suicide; boys are more likely to succeed.

Children and teens who have attempted suicide offer some interesting insights by sharing their innermost feelings and thoughts at the time they took this drastic step. The most common feelings reported by these children were anger, loneliness, worry about the future, failure, shame, and hopelessness. According to Dr. Cynthia Pfeffer (1983), who has written extensively on the subject of child and teen suicide, the most significant feeling is hopelessness.

Some of the reasons kids gave for considering suicide were:

- To escape from an impossible situation
- To make people understand how desperate they were feeling
- To make people feel sorry for the way they treated them
- To frighten people or otherwise get back at them

- To show how much they love someone
- To find out whether someone really loves them
- To be with a loved one who has died

As the parent of a depressed child, there are a number of important things to keep in mind that may help you lessen the chances of suicide.

- Every suicide threat should be taken seriously. You may think your child's suicidal statements or gestures are merely a means of getting your attention. So give it. The need is real; the risk is too.

- Don't pretend your child doesn't have suicidal thoughts. Otherwise he might go "underground" emotionally. Bear in mind that many suicide attempts are covert. Don't make your child feel guilty for having suicidal thoughts. Encourage him to come to you and talk openly.

- Listen to your child. Don't overlook passing comments or remarks that are seemingly made in jest.

- Validate your child's feelings. Don't diminish them with comments like, "You have so much to live for" or "You don't really want to kill yourself."

- Be alert to the following major suicide indicators and risk factors:

> Alcohol and/or drug abuse
> Slovenly appearance
> Pregnancy
> Physical illness or disability
> Running away
> Social isolation, loneliness
> Poor school performance or failure
> Loss of friends or status
> Anger and aggression
> Impulsivity
> Communication problems
> Perfectionism
> Suicide of another child or teen (suicides occur in clusters)
> Suicide threats or prior attempts
> Immediate access to a means to kill himself
> Loss of a loved one through death
> Family history of suicide
> Suddenly putting his affairs in order: giving away valued possessions, paying off debts, etc.

- Recognize that inpatient treatment may be required. A suicide attempt is a dramatic statement of how desperate your child is feeling. It may call for dramatic response on your part.

One parent shared the story of his teen daughter. When running away, drinking and skipping school failed to elicit the desired reaction from her parents, this very depressed young lady took what she considered to be the next logical step—an overdose of pills. Finally, someone sat up and took notice.

- Take suicide precautions:

  Remove firearms from the house immediately.
  Do not have a large supply of medications lying around.
  Dispense your child's medication and watch her take it.
  Have syrup of Ipecac available. This is an over-the-counter drug used to induce vomiting.

Depression and Substance Abuse

Substance abuse is closely associated with mood disorders. In one study, Drs. Frederick Goodwin and Kay Redfield Jamison (1990) found that in seven of ten cases of preadolescent alcohol abuse, the children were bipolar or cyclothymic (a less severe form of bipolar illness). The remaining three children had other forms of depressive illness.

Depression in childhood can easily escalate into substance abuse. Remember you're dealing with a child who already has damaged self-esteem, impaired judgement, and poor impulse control.

In some cases, a depressed child or teen may turn to drugs or alcohol in an attempt to self-medicate. Other reasons given for drinking or taking drugs include:

- Curiosity
- Escape
- Peer pressure
- Defiance

As a parent, you should be alert for the following signs of substance abuse:

- Sudden changes in mood or behavior
- Eyes that are red and bloodshot or dull and glazed
- Slurred speech
- Memory loss or mental confusion
- Changes in peer group
- Deteriorating schoolwork
- Truancy or disciplinary problems in school
- Lying, denying, and secretiveness
- Withdrawal from the family

- Changes in manner or dress or music
- Drugs or drug paraphernalia in the house or car

If you suspect or know that your child is drinking or taking drugs, deal with the problem head-on. Don't set your child up for a lie by asking, "Are you drinking or taking drugs?" Approach your child in a calm, straightforward manner. Tell him that you know, or have reason to believe, that he is using drugs or drinking. Seek professional help—immediately. Remember, depression, when compounded by drug or alcohol use, can increase your child's risk of suicide.

CHAPTER TEN

LOOKING TO THE FUTURE

I will never forget the day my family sat in Dr. Mary Jane Sale's office and reviewed the results of Nicholas' psychological tests. Finally, a diagnosis was confirmed—clinical depression. This followed more than eight years of wondering, blaming, worrying, and always suspecting that there was more to this child than the garden-variety ADHD that seems to be the diagnosis of choice for the '90s.

Contrary to what you might expect, I felt an incredible sense of relief. I decided if we could put a name to the problem, we could also find a solution.

My journey started in one bookstore and then another. Next came the library. After weeks of digging and scratching, with plenty of help from dozens of mental health professionals, I discovered many excellent resources. I then set about the task of learning what it's like to be a child coping with depression.

The more I learned, the more excited I became. Depression is not the dark, mysterious psychiatric ailment that I thought it to be. There is a wealth of current studies underway. New and exciting treatments. And a growing sense of awareness among educators, physicians and clinicians.

Yet, despite everything I learned, I can't help but wonder—no, make that worry—about my child's future. How will he fare in school? Will he be able to make friends? Will he find happiness? Will he survive the hormonal chaos of his teen years? Will I?

The odds are with us. I hang on tight to my favorite statistic. The 80 to 90 percent chance of a positive outcome for those depressed patients who receive treatment. My child is one of the lucky ones. He is in the hands of a skilled therapist. Has two parents who love him and a bunch of terrific teachers. But, most of all, he has the resilient spirit of a child.

All kids want to be happy. And with the kinds of help and hope that are available today through mental health research and the treatment community, the next generation may not have to face down the Turtle or the Dragon we now recognize as childhood depression.

FACTS ABOUT DEPRESSION

• In the United States, more than 15 million people suffer from depression each year.

• In this country, women have a 10 to 25 percent lifetime risk for major depression; men have a 5 to 12 percent lifetime risk.

• At any given time, from 5 to 9 percent of women are depressed and 2 to 3 percent of men.

• The onset of major depression can occur from childhood through old age, but 50 percent of patients have the onset between the ages of 20 and 50. Bipolar disorder begins somewhat earlier, the range being from childhood to 50, with a mean age of 30.

• Epidemiological data suggest that the age at onset is decreasing for those born more recently. Baby boomers are having increasingly higher incidence rates of depression.

• Major depression is an "equal opportunity disorder." Prevalence rates for depression are not affected by ethnicity, education, income, or marital status.

• Although mood disorders strike all races at an equal rate, there is a tendency for examiners to under-diagnose mood disorders and overdiagnose schizophrenia in patients who have a different racial or cultural background.

• Prior to the onset of puberty, boys and girls are equally affected. However, after puberty, females are twice as likely as males to develop a major depressive disorder. Although the reason for this difference is not known, there is speculation that it may be related to stresses, childbirth, learned helplessness, or hormonal effects.

• The financial implications of depression are great. In 1990, depression may have cost $30 billion, including $17 billion for loss of productivity in the workplace.

• Approximately 50 to 75 percent of depressed patients have impaired memory and concentration.

• Approximately 50 to 60 percent of individuals suffering a single episode of major depression can be expected to have a second episode. Individuals having two episodes have a 70 percent chance of having a third. And individuals who have had three episodes stand a 90 percent chance of having a fourth.

• Untreated episodes of depression usually last from six to 13 months. Treated episodes last approximately three months.

• It is estimated that 15 percent of untreated or inadequately treated depressives may eventually commit suicide. Among suicide victims, more than half are clinically depressed.

• About two thirds of all depressed patients think about suicide.

• Most bipolar patients are eventually seen by a physician, but it is estimated that only 20 to 25 percent of those who meet the criteria for major depression receive treatment.

• With appropriate treatment, 80 to 90 percent of even serious depressions can be alleviated.

RESOURCE GUIDE

BOOKS FOR CHILDREN

ADD-ADHD

ADHD: A Teenager's Guide
James J. Crist, Ph.D.
Plainview, NY: Childswork/Childsplay, LLC, 1996

Jumpin' Jake Settles Down
Lawrence E. Shapiro, Ph.D.
Plainview, NY: Childswork/Childsplay, LLC, 1994

Putting on the Brakes: Young People's Guide to Understanding Attention Deficit Hyperactivity Disorder (ADHD)
Patricia O. Quinn, M.D.
New York: Magination Press, 1991

Shelley the Hyperactive Turtle
Deborah M. Moss
Rockville, MD: Woodbine House, 1989

Sometimes I Drive My Mom Crazy, But I Know She's Crazy About Me: A Self-Esteem Book for ADHD Children
Lawrence E. Shapiro, Ph.D.
Plainview, NY: Childswork/Childsplay, LLC, 1993

ANGER

The Angry Monster Workbook
Hennie Shore
Plainview, NY: Childswork/Childsplay, LLC, 1995

Everything I Do You Blame on Me!:
A Book to Help Children Control Their Anger
Allyson Aborn, M.S.W., C.S.W.
Plainview, NY: Childswork/Childsplay, LLC, 1994

I Was So Mad!
Norma Simon
Morton Grove, IL: Albert Whitman, 1974

Sometimes I Like to Fight But I Don't Do It Much Anymore:
A Self-Esteem Book for Children with Difficulty in Controlling Their Anger
Lawrence E. Shapiro, Ph.D.
Plainview, NY: Childswork/Childsplay, LLC, 1995

The Very Angry Day That Amy Didn't Have
Lawrence E. Shapiro, Ph.D.
Plainview, NY: Childswork/Childsplay, LLC, 1995

When Emily Woke Up Angry
Riana Duncan
Barron's, 1989

COPING WITH DIVORCE

All About Divorce
Mary Blitzer Field
Plainview, NY: Childswork/Childsplay, LLC, 1992

The Boy's and Girl's Book About Divorce
Richard A. Gardner, M.D.
Jason Aronson: 1992

My Dad is Getting Married Again
Lisa M. Schab, L.C.S.W.
Plainview, NY: Childswork/Childsplay, LLC, 1996

My Life Turned Upside Down, But I Turned It Rightside Up
Mary Blitzer Field and Hennie Shore
Plainview, NY: Childswork/Childsplay, LLC, 1994

What Would You Do? A Child's Book About Divorce
Barbara Cain
Washington, DC: American Psychological Association, 1976

When Mom and Dad Separate: Children Can Learn to Cope with Grief from Divorce
Marge Haegaard

When Your Parents Get a Divorce: A Kid's Journal
Ann Banks
Puffin Books, 1990

DEPRESSION

Kid Power Tactics for Dealing with Depression
Nicholas & Susan E. Dubuque
Plainview, NY: Childswork/Childsplay, LLC, 1996

IMPULSIVITY AND SELF-CONTROL

The Girl's and Boy's Book About Good & Bad Behavior
Richard A. Gardner, M.D.
Cresskill, NJ: Creative Therapeutics, 1990

MAKING FRIENDS AND SOCIAL SKILLS DEVELOPMENT

The Best Friends Book
Sharon McCoy and Sheryl Scarborough
Lowell House Juvenile, 1995

Interactions
Debbie Pincus
Carthage, IL: Good Apple, 1988

Getting Along With My Friends
Tracy Zimmerman
Plainview, NY: Childswork/Childsplay, LLC, 1996

Making Friends
Kate Petty and Charlotte Firmin
Barron's, 1991

Manners Matter
Debbie Pincus
Carthage, IL: Good Apple, 1992

Sharing
Debbie Pincus
Carthage, IL: Good Apple, 1983

SELF-ESTEEM AND EMPOWERMENT

Anybody Can Bake a Cake
Hennie Shore, Beth Ann Marcozzi, and Lawrence E. Shapiro, Ph.D.
Plainview, NY: Childswork/Childsplay, LLC, 1996

The Building Blocks of Self-Esteem
Lawrence E. Shapiro, Ph.D.
Plainview, NY: Childswork/Childsplay, LLC, 1993

Don't Feed the Monster on Tuesday!: The Children's Self-Esteem Book
Adolph Moser, Ed.D.
Kansas City, MO: Landmark Editions, 19xx

Feeling Good About Others
Debbie Pincus
Carthage, IL: Good Apple, 1994

Feeling Good About Yourself
Debbie Pincus
Carthage, IL: Good Apple, 1990

How to Raise a Child With a High EQ
Lawrence E. Shapiro, Ph.D.
New York, NY: Harper Perennial, 1997

Let's Learn About Magnificent Me
Jeri A. Carroll
Carthage, IL: Good Apple, 1988

Getting Along With Myself
Hennie Shore
Plainview, NY: Childswork/Childsplay, LLC, 1996

My Best Friend Is Me!
Beth Ann Marcozzi
Plainview, NY: Childswork/Childsplay, LLC, 1995

Stick Up for Yourself! Every Kid's Guide to Personal Power and Positive Self-Esteem
Gershen Kaufman, Ph.D. and Lev Raphael, Ph.D.
Minneapolis: Free Spirit, 1990

STRESS MANAGEMENT

Coping: A Guide to Stress Management
Corinne Sanders and Cynthia Turner
Carthage, IL: Good Apple, 1983

Don't Pop Your Cork on Mondays!: The Children's Anti-Stress Book
Adolph Moser, Ed.D.
Kansas City, MO: Landmark Editions, 1980

Every Time I Blow My Top I Lose My Head
Laura Slap-Shelton, Psy.D. and Lawrence E Shapiro, Ph.D.
Plainview, NY: Childswork/Childsplay, LLC, 1992

THERAPY

A Child's First Book About Play Therapy
Marc A. Nemiroff, Ph.D.
Washington, DC: American Psychological Association, 1990

FEELINGS

All Feelings are OK: It's What You Do With Them That Counts
Lawrence E. Shapiro, Ph.D.
Plainview, NY: Childswork/Childsplay, LLC, 1993

Double-Dip Feelings: Stories to Help Children Understand Emotions
Barbara S. Cain, M.S.W.
New York: Magination Press, 1990

Face Your Feelings!
Plainview, NY: Childswork/Childsplay, LLC, 1993

Helping Children Understand Their Feelings
Joan Singleton Prestine
Carthage, IL: Good Apple, 1993

POSTERS, GAMES, TAPES, & MORE

POSTERS

Emotions Poster
Photos of children depicting 28 different emotions.
Plainview, NY: Childswork/Childsplay, LLC, 1992

Everyone Has Feelings Poster
Photos of people of all ages depicting 36 different emotions.
Plainview, NY: Childswork/Childsplay, LLC, 1995

GAMES

The Dinosaur's Journey to High Self-Esteem
Helps children learn to develop a meaningful, positive self-image.
Plainview, NY: Childswork/Childsplay, LLC, 1991

The Game of Change
Teaches children to cope with change.
Plainview, NY: Childswork/Childsplay, LLC, 2000

Mind Your Manners
Teaches the importance of manners for children.

Think on Your Feet
Helps children develop social skills while they solve common problems.
Plainview, NY: Childswork/Childsplay, LLC, 1998

The Ungame
Non-competitive game teaching sharing and listening skills.

TAPES

Discover the Four-Step Process to Maximize Your Child's Self-Esteem and Minimize Family Conflict
30-minute videotape and a workbook
Call 1-800-MY-KIDS5 (1-800-695-4375) for information.

Parenting for High Self-Esteem
Series of tapes on self-esteem, expressing feelings and discipline.

Many of the books, games and other teaching tools are available through Childswork/Childsplay, a Guidance Channel Company. A catalog can be requested by calling 1-800-962-1141. Please bear in mind that many of the items offered are designed for use by trained therapists. If you are unsure if a product is appropriate for home use, please ask. A customer service representative will assist you with your selections.

BOOKS FOR PARENTS, EDUCATORS, AND HELPING PROFESSIONALS

INFORMATIONAL RESOURCES

Finding Help-Finding Hope: A Guidebook to School Services for Families with a Child Who has Emotional, Behavioral or Mental Disorders
Winifred G. Anderson
The Federation of Families for Children's Mental Health, 1994

Taking Charge: A Handbook for Parents Whose Children Have Emotional Handicaps
Colleen Wagner, M.S.W., Editor
Portland, OR: Research and Training Center on Family Support and Children's Mental Health, Portland State University, 1994

DEPRESSION

Helping Your Depressed Child: A Reassuring Guide to the Causes and Treatments of Childhood and Adolescent Depression
Lawrence L. Kerns, M.D., with Adrienne B. Lieberman
Rockland, CA: Prima Publishing, 1993

Is Your Child Depressed?: If Your Child is Tired, Irritable, or Angry the Answer Might be "Yes"
Joel Herskowitz, M.D.
New York: Warner Books, 1990

The Optimistic Child: A Revolutionary Program that Safeguards Children Against Depression and Builds Lifelong Resilience
Martin E. P. Seligman, Ph.D.

You Mean I Don't Have to Feel This Way?: New Help for Depression, Anxiety, and Addiction
Colette Dowling
New York: Bantam Books, 1993

ADD-ADHD

The ADD Hyperactivity Workbook: For Parents, Teachers and Kids
Harvey C. Parker, Ph.D.
Plantation, FL: Impact Publications, 1988

The ADD Tool Kit
Ruth Gauchman and Abiel Wong
Plainview, NY: Childswork/Childsplay, LLC, 1994

Attention-Deficit Hyperactivity Disorder: A Handbook for Diagnosis and Treatment
Russell A. Barkley
New York: Guilford Press, 1990

Maybe You Know My Kid: A Parents' Guide to Identifying, Understanding and Helping Your Child With Attention-Deficit Hyperactivity Disorder
Mary Cahil Fowler
New York: Birch Lane Press, 1993

BEHAVIOR AND DISCIPLINE

Good Behavior: Over 1,200 Sensible Solutions to Your Child's Problems from Birth to Age Twelve
Stephen W. Garber, Ph.D., Marianne Dailes Garber, Ph.D. and Robyn Spizman
Fallbrook, CA: Family Life Productions, 1992

The Good Kid Book: How to Solve the 16 Most Common Behavior Problems
Howard N. Sloane
Research Press, 1988

Stop Struggling with Your Child
Evonne Weinhaus, M.A., and Karen Friedman, ACSW
New York: Harper Collins, 1991

Stop Struggling with Your Teen
Evonne Weinhaus, M.A., Karen Friedman, ACSW, and Judy Meyer
New York: Viking/Penguin, 1988

ANGER

Listen to Me, I'm Angry
Diedre Laiken and Alan Schneider
New York: Lothrop, Lee & Shepard, 1980

When Anger Hurts: Quieting the Storm Within
Matthew McKay, Ph.D., Peter D. Rogers, Ph.D. and Judith McKay, R.N.
Oakland, CA: New Harbinger Publications, 1989

COMMUNICATIONS SKILLS

How to Talk to Children About Really Important Things
Charles E. Schaefer, Ph.D.

How to Talk to Kids So Kids Will Listen & Listen So Kids Will Talk
Adele Faber and Elaine Mazlish
New York: Avon, 1980

STRESS MANAGEMENT

Stress and Your Child
Archibald D. Hart
Dallas: Word Publishers, 1992

Stress in Children: Common Sense Advice on How to Deal with Stress in Children of All Ages
Dr. Bettie B. Youngs

DIVORCE

The Parents Book About Divorce
Richard A. Gardner, M.D.
New York: Bantam Books, 1982

Associations and Organizations

National Alliance for the Mentally Ill
Colonial Place Three
2107 Wilson Blvd., Suite 300
Arlington, VA 22201-3042
(800) 950-NAMI (950-6264)
Help line for literature, information, and referral to local resources and support groups.

National Depressive and Manic Depressive Association
730 North Franklin, Suite 501
Chicago, IL 60610
(800) 82N-DMDA (826-3632)
Help line for referral to local agencies and support groups.

National Foundation for Depressive Illness
P.O. Box 2257
New York, NY 10116
(800) 248-4344
Recorded message that gives symptoms of depressive illnesses. You can write to request a list of physicians and support groups and a bibliography. They request a $5 donation (if you can afford to pay) and a self-addressed envelope to cover costs.

National Mental Health Association
1021 Prince Street
Alexandria, VA 22314
(800) 969-NMHA (969-6642)
Recorded message offering a materials on a wide array of mental health topics as well as a directory of local mental health associations. Information will be sent free of charge, but they ask for a contribution.

Depression Awareness, Recognition, and Treatment (D/ART)
National Institute of Mental Health
6001 Executive Blvd., Room 8184, MSC 9663
Bethesda, MD 20892-9663
(800) 421-4211
Recorded message offering free brochures on depression.

Federation of Families for Children's Mental Health
1021 Prince Street
Alexandria, VA 22314
703-684-7710
Call or write to request a list of names, addresses, and phone numbers of agencies in your state.

Research and Training Center on Family Support and Children's Mental Health
Portland State University
P.O. Box 751
Portland, OR 97207
(503) 725-4040
Call or write to request an order for for various books, brochures, and a state-by-state resource guide.

National Association of Anorexia Nervosa and Associated Disorders
P.O. Box 7
Highland Park, IL 600035
(708) 831-3438
Send a self-addressed stamped envelope or call for more information.

REFERENCES

Abramson, L.Y. et al. (1978) "Learned Helplessness in Humans: Critique and Reformulation." *Journal of Abnormal Psychology* 87: 47.

Akiskal, H.S., J. Downs, P. Jordan, S. Watson, D. Daugherty and D. Pruitt. (1985) "Affective Disorders in Referred Children and Younger Siblings of Manic-Depressives: Mode of Onset and Prospective Course." *Archives of General Psychiatry* 42: 996-1003.

American Psychiatric Association (1994) *Diagnostic and Statistical Manual of Mental Disorders,* Fourth Edition. Washington: DC: American Psychiatric Association Press.

Anderson, Winifred G. (1994) *Finding Help-Finding Hope: A Guidebook to School Services for Families With a Child who has Emotional, Behavioral or Mental Disorders.* Alexandria, VA: Federation of Families for Children's Mental Health.

Barkley, Russell A. (1990) *Attention-Deficit Hyperactivity Disorder: A Handbook for Diagnosis and Treatment.* New York: The Guilford Press.

Beck, Aaron T. et al. (1979) *Cognitive Therapy for Depression.* New York: Guilford Press.

Center for Mental Health Services. *Mental Health, United States, 1994.* Manderscheid, Ronald W. and Mary Anne Sonnenschein, eds. DHHS Pub. No. (SMA) 94-3000. Washington, D.C.: Supt. of Docs., U.S. Govt. Print. Off., 1994.

Delong, Robert (1990) "Lithium Treatment and Bipolar Disorders in Childhood." *North Carolina Medical Journal* 5, no.4 (April).

Depressive Illnesses: Treatments Bring New Hope. (1993) Rockville, MD: National Institute of Mental Health.

Dowling, Colette. (1991) *You Mean I Don't Have to Feel This Way? New Help for Depression, Anxiety, and Addiction.* New York: Scribner's.

Elkin, Irene. (1990) Interview in "Depression: Patients Get Younger as R_x Options Increase." *Medical World News* (April): 29-35.

Formanek, Ruth, and Anita Gurian, eds. (1987) *Women and Depression: A Lifespan Perspective.* New York: Springer Publishing Co.

Garfinkel, Barry D., Gabrielle A. Carlson and Elizabeth B. Weller. (1990) *Psychiatric Disorders in Children and Adolescents*. Philadelphia, PA: Harcourt, Brace, Jovanovich, Inc.

Gold, Mark S. (1987) *The Good News About Depression: Cures and Treatments in the New Age of Psychiatry*. New York: Villard Books.

Goodwin, Frederick and Kay Redfield Jamison. (1990) "Children and Adolescents," in *Manic Depressive Illness*. New York: Oxford University Press.

Gordon, Thomas. (1977) "Parent Effectiveness Training." Audiotape produced by *Psychology Today*.

Hawton, K. (1986) "Suicide and Attempted Suicide Among Children and Adolescents." *Developmental Psychology and Psychiatry*, vol. 5. Beverly Hills, CA: Sage Publications.

Herskowitz, Joel. (1988) *Is Your Child Depressed? If Your Child is Tired, Irritable, or Angry, the Answer May Be "Yes."* New York: Pharos Books.

Hirschfeld, Robert. (1991) *When the Blues Won't Go Away: New Approaches to Dysthymic Disorder and Other Forms of Chronic Low-Grade Depression*. New York: Macmillan.

Kaplan, Harold I. and Benjamin J. Sadock. (1988) *Synopsis of Psychiatry, Fifth Edition*. Baltimore, MD: Williams & Wilkins.

Karahasan, Alp. (1987) "Common Mental Illnesses: Symptoms and Treatment," in *Children and Adolescents with Mental Illness: A Parents Guide*. Evelyn McElroy, ed. Kensington, MD: Woodbine House.

Kashani, Javad H. et al. (1989) "Correlation of Suicidal Ideation in a Community Sample of Children and Adolescents," *Journal of Child and Adolescent Psychiatry* 28, no. 6, November.

Kelker, Katharin and Colleen Wagner, eds. (1994) *Taking Charge: A Handbook for Parents Whose Children Have Emotional Disorders*, 3rd Edition. Portland, OR: Portland State University, Research and Training Center on Family Support and Children's Mental Health.

Kerns, Lawrence L. with Adrienne B. Lieberman. (1993) *Helping Your Depressed Child: A Reassuring Guide to the Causes and Treatments of Childhood and Adolescent Depression.* Rocklin, CA: Prima Publishing.

Keys, A. et al. (1950) *The Biology of Human Starvation.* Minneapolis: University of Minneapolis Press.

Klein, Rachael G. and Cheryl Slomkowski. (1993) "Treatment of Psychiatric Disorders in Children and Adolescents." *Psychopharmacology Bulletin* 29: 525-535.

Klerman, Gerald L. and Myrna M. Weissman. (1989) "Increasing Rates of Depression." *Journal of the American Medical Association* 261: 2229-2235.

Klerman, Gerald L., Myrna M. Weissman, Bruce J. Rounsaville and Eve S. Chevron. (1984) *Interpersonal Psychotherapy of Depression.* New York: Basic Books.

Kovacs, Maria (1985) "The Natural History and Course of Depressive Disorders in Childhood." *Psychiatric Annals* .

Lewis, Melvin, ed. (1991) *Child and Adolescent Psychiatry: A Comprehensive Textbook.* Baltimore, MD: Williams & Wilkins.

Let's Talk About Depression. (1991) DHHS Pub. No. (ADM) 91-1695. Washington, D.C.: Supt. of Docs., U.S. Govt. Print. Off.

McElroy, Evelyn, ed. (1987) *Children and Adolescents with Mental Illness: A Parent's Guide.* Kensington, MD: Woodbine House.

McKnew, Jr., Donald H. and Leon Cytryn and Herbert Yahraes. (1983) *Why Isn't Johnny Crying: Coping with Depression in Children.* New York: W.W. Norton & Company.

Mondimore, Francis M. (1990) *Depression: The Mood Disease.* Baltimore, MD: The Johns Hopkins University Press.

Munir, Kerim. (1989) "Child and Adolescent Pharmacotherapy Comes of Age" in *Psychotherapist's Guide to Pharmacotherapy,* ed. James M. Ellison. Chicago: Yearbook Medical Publishers.

Pfeffer, Cynthia. (1983) *The Suicidal Child.* New York: Guilford Press.

Plain Talk About Dealing with the Angry Child. (1978) Rockville, MD: National Institute of Mental Health.

Puig-Antich, Joaquim et al. (1985) "Psychosocial Functioning in Prepubertal Major Depressive Disorders." *Archives of General Psychiatry* 42: 500-573.

Puig-Antich, Joaquim and Burt Weston. (1983) "The Diagnosis and Treatment of Major Depressive Disorders in Childhood." *Annual Review of Medicine* 34: 231-45.

Robins, Lee N. and Darrel A. Regier, eds. (1991) *Psychiatric Disorders in America*. New York: Free Press.

Rosenthal, P.A. and S. Rosenthal. (1982) "Fact of Fallacy of Preschool-Age Suicide." Paper presented at the Annual Meeting of the APA, Toronto, May 1982.

Rush, John. (1985) *Beating Depression*. New York: Facts on File.

Sargent, Marilyn. (1994) *Plain Talk About Depression*. Rockville, MD: National Institute of Mental Health.

Saunders, Antoinette and Bonnie Remsberg. (1984) *The Stressproof Child: A Loving Parents' Guide*. New York: Holt, Rinehart and Winston.

Seligman, Martin E.P., Karen Reivich, Lisa Jaycox and Jane Gillham. (1995) *The Optimistic Child: A Revolutionary Program that Safeguards Children Against Depression and Builds Lifelong Resilience*. Boston: Houghton Mifflin.

Seligman, M.E. and C.A. Peterson. (1982) "A Learned Helplessness Perspective on Childhood Depression: Theory and Research." Paper presented at Social Science Research Council Conference on Depressive Disorders: Developmental Perspective, Philadelphia, April 1982.

Spitz, Rene A.(1946) "Anaclitic Depression: An Enquiry into the Genesis of Psychiatric Conditions in Early Childhood." *Psychoanalytic Study of the Child* 2: 313.

Stark, Kevin. (1994) Interview in *The Child Therapy News*. Childswork/Childsplay, LLC, vol.I, no.4 (April).

The Child Therapy News. (1994) Childswork/Childsplay, LLC, vol.I, no.4 (April).

Thomas, Patricia. (1990) "Depression: Patients Get Younger as R_x Options Increase." *Medical World News* (April): 29-35.

What To Do When a Friend is Depressed: Guide for Students. (1994) National Institute for Mental Health Publication, No. 94-3824.

Vail, Priscilla L. (1987) *Smart Kids With School Problems.* New York: E.P. Dutton.

Weinhaus, Evonne and Karen Friedman. (1991) *Stop Struggling with Your Child.* New York: Harper Perennial.

Werkman, Sidney. (1993) "The Role of Medication." *Journal of EB-P* (Summer): 42-44.

STAY IN TOUCH

During the course of researching and writing this book, I spoke to hundreds of parents from around the country. Now, I'd love to hear from you. Please take a minute to share your experiences, thoughts and suggestions. Perhaps the most important parent survival strategy of all is working together.

How was A Parent's Survival Guide to Childhood Depression *helpful to you and your family?*

What additional information would have been helpful to you?

What experiences have you had–the good, the bad and the ugly–that you would like to share?

Please e-mail Susan Dubuque at

sdubuque@neathawkdubuque.com

Susan Dubuque and her son, Nicholas, have also written a book just for kids – it's called *Kid Power Tactics for Dealing with Depression*. *Kid Power Tactics* helps children understand depression – what it is, what causes it and how it is treated. They'll learn practical strategies for dealing with everyday problems – from feeling embarrassed, to making friends, to controlling anger. *Kid Power Tactics* is easy to read – because it's written in 'kid-talk' – and fun to use.

Kid Power Tactics for Dealing with Depression is published by Childswork/Childsplay, LLC, Plainview, NY, and can be ordered by calling 1-800-962-1141

ABOUT THE AUTHOR

Susan Dubuque holds a Bachelor of Arts degree in Psychology from East Stroudsburg University, East Stroudsburg, PA, and a Master's degree in Counseling from Lehigh University, Bethlehem, PA. She is president and co-founder of MSI, a healthcare marketing and public relations firm in Richmond, VA.